DEMAND

TRANSPARENCY

Stop Wall Street Greed and Rising Taxes
From Destroying Your Wealth

By

JASON G. MANDEL

Performance Publishing
McKinney, TX

ISBN 978-1-956914-94-8 paperback
ISBN 978-1-956914-91-7 hardcover
ISBN 978-1-956914-88-7 ebook

CONTENTS

DEDICATION

To my grandfather, Maxwell Goldpin, in honor of his one hundredth birthday: I dedicate this book to you because you have taught me how to live a balanced life focused on our family's core beliefs in honesty, integrity, faith, patriotism and the unconditional love of family and friends.

To my father Jack (of blessed memory): You inspired me to write this book and share my views. I hope this book encourages people to take action the way that your books were able to. You left us too soon but your memory lives on through your children and grandchildren who miss you very much.

THANK YOU

I thank the following people for their support and love during the process of writing this book: my wife Dana, my children Grant and Skylar, my brothers Joshua, Jordan and Jaron and my devoted mother Ronni. The love you share with me each day motivates me to be the best version of myself.

I also want to give a special nod of appreciation to Lewis Fein, for his advice and counsel since our college days. Thank you for all your help with this book and I could not have gotten it done without you.

Finally, I want to thank my dear friend Dr. Woojin Kim who inspired me to take better care of my health and be more aware of the blessings that G-d has bestowed on me.

Thank you.

FOREWORD

By Ben Stein

Increases in the speed of information have no influence on the reliability of information.

How markets react to information, rising or falling in a flash; how information comes in waves, displacing individual and institutional investors, until this tsunami of data hits a billion-plus devices and registers as a cacophony of sounds, of vibrations from within and without, in which our smartphones and tablets move like sentient but soulless machines; how machines move markets, in response to preprogrammed orders to buy or sell on specific information, regardless of the source of information, is how we live now.

Financial diversification is how an investor survives this turmoil, succeeding over time without panicking in times of uncertainty, because few things in life are certain.

What is certain, despite the protestations of those who see themselves as gods and see no reason, based on their own narrow aperture of reason, to believe in G-d, for they believe technology will deliver them not only from Earth—to life on another planet—but from the earth from which they were taken, is that we are all mortal; we shall all return to dust.

How we choose to live, that we are free to choose, is critical to how well we may live during the remaining days of our years.

How we choose to invest is no less important to our posterity, so future generations may enjoy the blessings of financial security.

I said as much twenty years ago in a primer and self-help book of my own, *How to Ruin Your Financial Life*[1].

The author of this book, Jason Mandel, is a fan of that book, my book, which he calls his "Israeli passport."

Jason's chapter on the miracle of Israel would not exist but for the sacrifices of the greatest savior of Israel, save the Jewish Lord and Savior of the Christian Bible, whose memory is a blessing to Jews throughout the Holy Land.

I refer, of course, to President Richard M. Nixon, who risked everything—and gave Prime Minister Golda Meir everything she needed—to prevent a second Holocaust.

My late father, Herbert Stein, chairman of the Council of Economic Advisers under Mr. Nixon, performed a separate miracle in guiding Israel to a stable currency and market economy.

Two miracle workers, Mr. Nixon and my father, whose works are a testament to a people with an everlasting name.

In the name of security, for the virtue of security, be forever vigilant about how you live your financial life too.

Jason repeats this point, explaining the benefits of life insurance and decentralized finance (DeFi).

---

1 Stein, Ben. (2004). *How to Ruin Your Financial Life*. Hay House Inc. https://a.co/d/7XsYMh0

From investing in a principal-protected life insurance policy to reducing or eliminating taxable income with life insurance, Jason is clear and persuasive.

He brings the same clarity to financial technology, highlighting the rewards of innovation—of how innovation works—and of how innovation rewards workers by lowering costs, expediting transactions, and increasing remittances worldwide.

Pointed in his analysis, and poignant in his most personal moments, Jason's story also gives me hope that we shall nobly save the last best hope of earth.

AUTHOR'S NOTE

> **"The legacy of heroes is the memory of a great name and the inheritance of a great example."**
>
> —Benjamin Disraeli

Three miles from my childhood home, the flags of church and state fly from the same pole—the flag of the United States flying above the flag of the Episcopal Church. These two flags grace the grounds of Grace Episcopal Church in Massapequa, New York.

The colors evoke the sacredness of honor and the power of sacrifice, of death in war and the death of a martyr for peace, of our independence from and indebtedness to England.

Outside Old Grace Church, history resounds from the square bell tower with a spire, summoning citizens of all faiths to gather round crosses and Stars of David. The summons is both a call to prayer and a prelude to a moment of silence. Here, we may mourn the fallen and resolve that these dead shall not have died in vain.

And in silence comes the promise of the nation's savior.

His pledge goes on, just as his name lives on. For the memory of Abraham Lincoln inspires us to care for him who shall have borne the battle and for his widow and his orphan. By continuing his work—and I do not pretend to be worthy of standing anywhere but *far* behind the shadow of his greatest works—with reverence for his charity and gratitude toward his magnanimity, I hope to be true to his name.

If this book inspires people to care enough to act, such that the care they want is the care they receive, then all the better. And if this book inspires people to care enough to ask before acting, such that the care they have is the care they want, then even better.

This book reflects the concerns I have, starting with the reasons why I care about the life of my country and the lives of my countrymen. Because liberty without security is perilous, and freedom without opportunity is precarious, financial independence is essential. Financial independence is real—provided we choose not only to pursue it, but to purchase it.

We have a duty to get all the life insurance we need. In doing so, we may give our posterity a legacy to preserve, protect, and defend. The legacy we create—born in the present and bearing interest for the rest of our tomorrows—is the memorial we invite future generations to perpetuate.

My memorial is in the pages of this book, in tribute to the people and principles responsible for this book.

My interest is in the principle of principal itself—of showing people how to safeguard their money and earn tax-free income. I created the Mandel Family Office to give back and help others properly protect their own families, as I have done for my own. I post content on social media to help everyone learn my strategies, as serving only the wealthy is not fair to those without access to best in class advice and counsel. I personally respond to questions sent to my email address (jason@themandelfamilyoffice.com) or text messages sent to the same phone number (917.603.2365), which I have had since 1999 when I started my first firm. I do not discriminate based on the net worth of the person contacting me, and I share my opinions with anyone seeking out investment transparency and knowledge.

My legacy is in the use of this book as a guidebook. And my goal is to lead people to that which is attainable: financial security, in whole or in part, through a combination of radical transparency and freedom of choice.

May we have the wisdom to choose the path to financial independence and security.

May we have the will to follow the path till the end, so we may achieve the ends we deserve while establishing a legacy worth defending.

INTRODUCTION

Tents fill the encampments while people crowd the fields. The people constitute a tent city within the larger city, evoking images of foreign cities in which extreme poverty competes with extreme wealth.

Such is life in a great American city.

Such is the nature too of a national tragedy, bringing plague to a land that stretches from California to New York.

And yet the land looks the way it does, vulgar and unsafe, because of the belief that the "new normal" is normal. That it is okay to replace laws and the words that give meaning to the laws we observe with orders—arbitrary orders—that force businesses to close and residents to flee. That it is okay to bankrupt small business owners and burden the nation with $28.43 trillion in debt, a debt the nation cannot retire and which makes it all the more difficult for Americans *to* retire. That it is okay to live in fear—to suffer nameless, unjustified terror—while violent criminals run free.

The scene repeats itself in city after city, minus changes in scenery. There are palm trees set like vertical blinds before a picture window of Los Angeles, filtering daylight in shades of pink and gold. There is a profusion of artificial light in Miami, coloring downtown red, yellow, and white. There are ghost lights along the

Great White Way, while Chicago is in darkness and San Francisco suffers in distress.

The scene is no better inland, where waves of grain move as ocean waves—the wind tearing apart families as it tears through family farms.

If the lights are to return, we must imbue our minds with the lights of truth. I am aware that my life is but a flicker among the flames of knowledge. But to the extent that I can help, I am happy to carry the torch. I am happy to bring the lights to citizens and communities nationwide, enlightening readers via this book.

Born of decades of professional experience and borne by my personal experiences during a day of fire on September 11, 2001, I strive to temper the sternness of today with the safety of tomorrow. In this book, I explain how investors can minimize risk with principal-protected life insurance strategies and how they can invest in venture-backed startups and other non-correlated investment strategies.

Explaining how to balance risk is why I enjoy my work.

This work—not the work I did on Wall Street—is my vocation. It is a calling to inform and inspire, thus honoring my father by following his example without following in his footsteps. For I chart a separate path to the same goal.

About my father, to whom I owe so much, I have more to say.

About my work on Wall Street—about what I learned versus what I earned, though I earned plenty—I say what I believe: People should not place all their retirement savings in investments over which they have no control.

Most questions about financial performance are unanswerable, and the only honest answer is to say that performance is unknowable in advance. For that reason, I choose to work with what I know, based on what I can guarantee, according to what my clients and all people can see for themselves. By that, I mean I'm transparent about the terms and conditions of a life insurance contract.

What a contract allows an owner to do is not a matter of conjecture. Power belongs to the person who holds the pen and signs a contract, not the broker who deals in hyperbole or the salesman who engages in double-dealing. Power goes where it belongs, reserving to each man or woman what the Constitution delegates to all people: those powers not prohibited by a contract. The language differs, as do the laws governing contracts. But the principle—the idea that the truth of a proposition is in the text of a proposition—is similar.

But when the manipulation of words is no different than the manipulation of dollars, thus breaking the bank of social trust and straining if not severing the bonds of affection, the people are right to distrust Wall Street.

If we are to do right by the people, we must first begin to understand the wrongs done to the people. For all history is not the history of class struggles, but rather the history of peoples struggling—yearning—to speak to the living.

The speakers communicate through a telegraphy system of the soul. Thus, the pressure of feet on pavement absorbs the pulses of history, making every man a medium for a message from the realm of the Wall Street Historic District.

This district consists of canyons and shadows, where buildings stand as monuments to capital and a monument to a man stands outside the nation's first capital. Where the House of Morgan borders 15 Broad Street and a statue stands outside 26 Wall Street, icons of honor and faith endure.

Here, a bronze sculpture of George Washington stands as a symbol of virtue while a gilded cross stands atop a haven from vice, leading people from the valley of trade, the trading of money and goods and services, toward the house of the Lord. These symbols offer all G-d's children—black men and white men, Jews and Gentiles, Protestants and Catholics—a respite from cruelty and pain.

In this house, the house of the father, there are many mansions. And from this house, a lighthouse of salvation, shines the light of the world. The light emanates from the chancel window of Trinity Church at the intersection of Wall Street and Broadway, where figures of Christendom stand like Samaritans, showing mercy and sheltering people from terror.

The church stands as a survivor of the September 11 attacks, with a pew—the only surviving pew from the day of the attacks—as a row of remembrance. It is in remembrance of all who sought and received refuge from a cloud that dimmed, but did not destroy, the twin lights of faith and freedom.

On that day, as my brother walked to my apartment in a shroud of dust and debris, after he buried his clothes and washed the dead from his body, I looked for the light.

I looked for the light to guide the lost and guard the good.

I looked for Wall Street to see the light.

*

"Wall Street sells stocks and bonds, but what it really peddles is hope."

—Jason Zweig, *The Devil's Financial Dictionary*

But for an adviser here or an analyst there, but for a person with the means—the financial independence—to speak truth to power, the powers that be ration the flow of information. And save for a person who sounds the alarm—whose conscience rings louder than the opening or closing bell on Wall Street—the many are silent.

Silence is a form of tax retention, where an investment firm withholds information. Silence is also an example of uninformed consent, where a firm does not volunteer what it has no legal duty to disclose: that an investment product is not necessarily the best available product.

However, no client should hesitate to ask if a comparable or less expensive product exists. Regardless of the reason—whether due to feelings of fear or pride—not asking the question and knowing the answer, for fear of causing insult or injury, is an act of self-harm.

No one expects a client to know the intricacies of finance or the mechanics of a financial product. But every client has a right to know how an adviser makes money, because every transaction makes money for an adviser. This fact, that what is good for an adviser is not always good for a client, puts a client at a disadvantage.

Even if an adviser takes a fee instead of a commission, his goal is to keep and expand his list of clients. His goal is to make more money by having more money to invest, regardless of how his investments perform. His business is to minimize redemptions, not maximize returns for investors. Because anything that prompts investors to sell causes an adviser to lose money.

Better for an adviser to do as Ray Dalio[2] says and adopt a policy of "radical transparency" rather than do a disservice to investors.

---

2 Principles by Dalio. (2018, May 2). *Why radical truth and radical transparency are keys to success* [Video]. YouTube. https://youtu.be/7KqyXF9f1dc

To realize this right is to exercise the right to execute a transaction without interference. It's a right to writing contracts—smart contracts—that anyone can audit but no one can alter.

To be one of two parties to an agreement, and to do business without a third party, is to eliminate the fees banks charge to process a transaction. And to do these things by decentralizing finance, with the tools of decentralized finance (DeFi)[3], is to defy how financial institutions do business.

Without such means, an investor may choose to forgo business. They may refrain from wiring funds or funding an investment by writing a check. They may avoid overriding the checks that protect the people with a check, thus upsetting the balances of justice. Or they may neglect that which will put an account in arrears, leaving an investor with a negative balance in their checking account and no further checks against bankruptcy.

Recall what Ben Bradlee (Jason Robards) says in the film *All the President's Men*, directed by Alan J. Pakula and based on Woodward and Bernstein's nonfiction book of the same name.

If you have not seen the film, please rent or buy it immediately. Watch it in its entirety, but focus on the scene[4] between Bradlee, Bob Woodward (Robert Redford), and Carl Bernstein (Dustin Hoffman), in which Bradlee, executive editor of the *Washington Post*, says, "I can't do the reporting for my reporters, which means I have to trust them. And I hate trusting anybody."

---

3 Schär, Fabian. "Decentralized Finance: On Blockchain- and Smart Contract-Based Financial Markets." *Review*, vol. 103, no. 2, 2021, pp. 153-174. https://fi les.stlouisfed.org/files/htdocs/publications/review/2021/04/15/full-issue.pdf

4 *All the President's Men*. Directed by Alan J. Pakula, performances by Jason Robards, Dustin Hoffman, and Robert Redford, Warner Bros., 1976. YouTube, uploaded by Movieclips, 20 October 2012 https://youtu.be/Tg4_lfm5VrQ

Do as Bradlee said, not as he did. For Woodward and Bernstein displayed questionable journalistic ethics, denying for decades what Barry Sussman,[5] the *Post's* Watergate editor, said he has known for a long time: that an anonymous source ("Z") was a grand juror,[6] not a worker inside the Nixon White House or a member of Nixon's reelection campaign.

About Woodward's meetings with the Watergate informant "Deep Throat," Bradlee[7] would later say, "There's a residual fear in my soul that that isn't quite straight."

Consider, too, that it was Woodward who, eight years after the *Post* won the Pulitzer Prize for Public Service for its investigation

---

5 Sussman, Barry. "How Woodward and Bernstein Came to Interview Grand Jurors." *HuffPost*, 4 May 2012, www.huffingtonpost.com/barry-sussman/woodward-bernstein-grand-juror_b_1478282.html

6 Rosen, James. "Why Bradleegate Matters: Woodward and Bernstein's Deception." *The Atlantic*, 22 May 2012, www.theatlantic.com/politics/archive/2012/05/why-bradleegate-matters-woodward-and-bernsteins-deception/257487/

7 Holland, Max. "New Questions About Deep Throat in 'All the President's Men': Watergate Revisited." *The Daily Beast*, 1 May 2012, www.thedailybeast.com/articles/2012/05/01/new-questions-about-deep-throat-in-all-the-president-s-men-watergate-revisited

of the Watergate case, submitted Janet Cooke's[8] story ("Jimmy's World") for the Pulitzer Prize for Feature Writing.

Cooke won and subsequently returned the prize, because her story of a third-generation heroin addict—an eight-year-old boy named Jimmy—was a lie.

So yes, Bradlee was right not to trust anybody. That he did not follow his own advice speaks to the dangers of entrusting others. His decision led to a condoning of unethical conduct by journalists to expose corrupt and illegal conduct among politicians. After all, diligence in the defense of accuracy is incompatible with recklessness in the pursuit of deadlines.

Or perhaps profits born of falsehoods are akin to false prophets borne with guilt: unsustainable.

Today, the *Post* is a more partisan and less profitable institution—so much so that its original owner no longer exists, and its principal shareholder (Warren Buffett) no longer owns any stock in the company.

[8] Sager, Mike. "The fabulist who changed journalism." *Columbia Journalism Review*, Spring 2016, www.cjr.org/the_feature/the_fabulist_who_changed_journalism.php

In 1973, Buffett paid $10 million for a 10 percent stake in the Washington Post Company. In 2014, after Jeff Bezos bought the paper for $250 million, Buffett exchanged his shares,[9] tax-free, for $1.1 billion in Berkshire Hathaway stock, ownership of ABC affiliate WPLG-TV in Miami, and cash.

Despite an 11,000 percent return over forty-one years, or an average annual increase of 268 percent, Buffett left a *lot* of money on the table. His success contradicts his own advice, as he excludes time from his philosophy of investing[10], saying, "[our] favorite holding period is forever."

The problem with forever is that—notwithstanding that which is immortal yet immaterial, excluding faith in eternal life—nothing lasts forever.

Had you bought 100 shares of the Washington Post Company on December 29, 2004, at the closing high of $996.74,[11] it would have taken ten years to break even, when the renamed Graham Holdings closed at $1,000.09, on February 18, 2015.

Presuming you had not sold the stock when it fell to $316 in 2011, and presuming you intend to hold your shares forever, your $100,000 investment would have been worth almost $60,000 by the end of 2022.

---

9 Yang, Jia Lynn, and Steven Mufson. "Warren Buffett in negotiations to relinquish $1.1 billion stake in Graham Holdings." *Washington Post*, 13 February 2014, www.washingtonpost.com/business/economy/warren-buffett-in-negotiations-to-relinquish-11billion-stake-in-graham-holdings/2014/02/13/bf6d0a92-94f8-11e3-83b9-1f024193bb84_story.html

10 Berkshire Hathaway Inc. (1989). *Annual report*. Retrieved from www.berkshirehathaway.com/letters/1988.html

11 Sloan, Allan. "Graham Holdings' new high a surprise 10 years after its last one ." *Washington Post*, 19 February 2015, www.washingtonpost.com/business/economy/graham-holdings-new-high-a-surprise-10-years-after-its-last-one/2015/02/19/37a4a982-b87c-11e4-a200-c008a01a6692_story.html

These points are important because people trust what Warren Buffett says. And at the same time, Buffett says he does not invest in what he does not know.

To wit, critics should ask Buffett why he continued to own investments ravaged by the very thing he refused to invest in: technology. He watched the Washington Post Company's "economic moat" become a morass—a sinkhole—of layoffs and losses. And he did not watch the people whose job it was to protect the moat.

The people who ran the company let the moat narrow until the fortress lay defenseless—until the siege forced the sale of *Newsweek*[12] for a dollar, plus $47 million in liabilities.

For decades the company's people watched technology weaken print and electronic media. They watched what cable had done to television and what a network of coaxial cables did to network TV, reducing the power of the "Big Three" networks by surpassing them altogether.

They watched as 105 million[13] households paid to watch cable TV.

They watched but did not see the light, as glass replaced copper, translating data into pulses of light.

They watched the rise of cable news and the purchase of *Newsweek's* competitor by a technology company.

They watched *Time* pass, as its circulation declined and its value dropped.

---

12 Newsweek staff. "The Washington Post Company Agrees to Sell NEWSWEEK to Sidney Harman." *Newsweek*, 2 August 2010, www.newsweek.com/washington-post-company-agrees-sell-newsweek-sidney-harman-71647

13 Ricca, Charlotte. "OTT disrupted cable television and film. Is the news next?" *Digital Content Next*, 11 March 2021, www.digitalcontentnext.org/blog/2021/03/11/ott-disrupted-cable-television-and-film-is-the-news-next/

They watched as the stock market[14] said the *Post* was worthless, that its valuation was zero.

They watched analog die and digital thrive, while inviting us to watch Bob Woodward and Ben Bradlee read the *Post* on an iPad.[15]

They should have invited us to watch the two eulogize the *Post* instead—or do anything but deliver an ode to the past in the code of the present, in a medium they did not understand.

They—the deans and doyennes of the *Post*—did nothing because they believed they had done nothing wrong. They acted according to their beliefs, as if they were the guardians of a regional aristocracy and the chosen representatives of the old guard. They oversaw one of the fourth estate's largest properties: a mid-Atlantic kingdom of newspapers, magazines, and TV stations.

They commanded the heights of power, in the Heights[16] alongside the powerful, with commanding views of the nation's capital and the Potomac below, whence the river flows through Washington, D.C., resounding with the currents of history, from the charge of the Army of the Potomac to the course of a former commander in chief; reverberating with the voices of Roosevelt, Truman, Eisenhower, Kennedy, Johnson, and Nixon; recalling the company of presidents and prime ministers, and of friends and countrymen, until the sound of the coxswain echoes from the boathouse outside Georgetown University.

---

14 Lee, Timothy B. "The stock market thinks the Washington Post is worth around $0 ." *Washington Post*, 6 August 2013, www.washingtonpost.com/news/the-switch/wp/2013/08/06/the-stock-market-thinks-the-washington-post-is-worth-around-0/

15 Washington Post. (2010, November 8). *The Washington Post App for iPad* [Video]. YouTube. https://youtu.be/KCUFxFoaloE

16 Fletcher, Carlton. "Georgetown Heights." *Glover Park History*, www.gloverparkhistory.com/geography/maps-places-features/georgetown-heights/

The sound awakens us to reality, so we may chart the outflow of capital and see what ruined the *Post*. And what sank the *Post* is sunk cost fallacy.[17]

"The sunk cost effect is the general tendency for people to continue an endeavor, or continue consuming or pursuing an option, if they've invested time or money or some resource in it," says Christopher Olivola, an assistant professor of marketing at Carnegie Mellon's Tepper School of Business and the author of a 2018 paper[18] on the topic published in the journal *Psychological Science*.

With respect to Professor Olivola, the truth of this fallacy is everywhere. It is in the air, in clouds of cigarette smoke beneath which a gambler's money goes up in flames. It is in the smoke and chaos of war, where no battle plan ever survives the first encounter with the enemy.

The truth is in the smoke—the steam—of hot air, which we tell ourselves to justify our bad investments.

With respect to Warren Buffett, the fallacy is that duty is discretionary and diligence dispensable. His conduct sounds more like actionable misconduct, with regard to Berkshire Hathaway's purchase of McLane,[19] a $50 billion-plus provider of supply chain solutions. He says he closed the deal in two hours, with no diligence save a phone call and a handshake.

Either Buffett believes most people are good, or he thinks most people believe a good story. His story sounds too good to be true.

---

[17] Ducharme, Jamie. "The Sunk Cost Fallacy Is Ruining Your Decisions. Here's How." *Time*, 26 July 2018, www.time.com/5347133/sunk-cost-fallacy-decisions/

[18] Olivola, Christopher Y. "The Interpersonal Sunk-Cost Effect." *Psychological Science*, vol. 29, no. 7, 2018, www.doi.org/10.1177/0956797617752641

[19] Berkshire Hathaway Inc. (2004). *Annual Report*. Retrieved from www.berkshirehathaway.com/letters/2003ltr.pdf

The fact is, most people want to believe Buffett is good, that he is not only a value investor but an investor whose values are sound. That he is a man of the people—the people's billionaire—who represents the triumph of Main Street over the tumult of Wall Street. That he is rich but not ruthless.

Or maybe he wants people to believe he is wise and almost never wrong. That he is in but not of the new Gilded Age. That he is more of a storyteller like Mark Twain than a character in one of Twain's stories. That the twain do meet, that they share a name, with Buffett born near the banks of the Missouri River and Twain born in the state of Missouri.

Trust that the real story is more complex than Buffett would have us believe. Trust that money is like power—that money *is* power—because power tends to corrupt. And remember that the powerful are loath to relinquish power, that the monopolization of power is powerful, that the history of the nation's trusts is the history of violations of the public trust.

Trust that history does not end, that it is an argument without end, and that time silences the players without stopping the performance. Trust that the just are few, the complacent many, and the transcendent as rare as the faces on Mount Rushmore.

We can argue about trust, or we can trust that transparency settles most arguments. Or we can do as the store man says: trust no one or nothing without proof.

So says the salesman to Tony Manero (John Travolta) in the opening credits of *Saturday Night Fever*.[20]

---

[20] *Saturday Night Fever*. Directed by John Badham, opening credits, Paramount Pictures, 1977. YouTube, uploaded by skyMTV, 26 January 2018 https://youtu.be/HVEqy6K18Yo

TONY MANERO
Alright, look, I wanna put down five dollars for the blue shirt in the window.

HABERDASHERY SALESMAN
Hey, wait for your receipt.

TONY MANERO
I trust you.

HABERDASHERY SALESMAN
Please, no, don't trust me.

*

"Dramatic and emotional trading experiences tend to be negative. Pride is a great banana peel, as are hope, fear, and greed. My biggest slip-ups occurred shortly after I got emotionally involved with positions."

—Ed Seykota, *Market Wizards: Interviews with Top Traders*

Man is by nature a political animal and an emotional creature. And he is able, but not always willing, to match his words with his actions.

No man is always rational and just, nor is he right in his logic and sound in his judgment. If this were the case, all mankind would be peaceful and free. All free markets would be transparent, fair, and efficient.

Man is predictably unpredictable, which is why volatility is as natural to man as it is an immutable part of nature. And this truth—that all men contain multitudes, that from many we are not always one—makes us human.

But humanness is not proof of humaneness, just as knowledge of good and evil does not make all men good. Because knowledge confers power, not prudence. Knowledge frees us to choose to honor G-d or believe we are gods.

By this power, and with the power to slip the surly bonds of Earth, man has the power to see the nature of man and the volatility of nature. Man also has the power to see what binds us together. Because the ties that bind us to life—be they cords of strength or chords of memory—stretch from the past to the present and future.

The ties weather the strain of passion, just as man endures his own trial by weather. For volatility is everywhere, in everything, during seasons of want and plenty and months of cold and heat.

As volatility varies, so too does man's tolerance for volatility. And what a person can survive is different from what his portfolio can sustain: extreme volatility.

Some volatility is acceptable. But total and extreme volatility is intolerable. For this reason, variety is desirable and diversification advisable. Such is the reasoning behind indexing, tax mitigation, low fees, and principal-protected investments within a life insurance contract.

Protection from volatility in trading also depends on protection from volatile traders. After all, Wall Street is no stranger to addiction. If the work drives people to drink, and if the drive to get ahead causes people to drink and do drugs, imagine how the public would respond to this news.

And yet this fact—that alcohol and drug addiction[21] is endemic to Wall Street—is not new. The fact lends itself to the depiction of a trading house as a drug house in which the chief commodity is cocaine rather than commodity futures. This reinforces the idea—the lie—that a trader has no future unless he is a high-functioning drug addict.

And that people choose to *exaggerate* these facts is why drug abuse in the financial industry gets a pass. It's as if it is okay to poison yourself—but not kill yourself—provided you make a killing on Wall Street. And you must keep making money, because the totality of your worth as an individual is your net worth.

This mindset is no less dangerous than any combination of mind-altering drugs.

As the nature of most work on Wall Street is long and hard, and as the work expands and stress increases, an already unhealthy situation worsens. The situation is competitive to the point of absurdity, resulting in a war of all against all, until what the winner gains is the interest he bears: a debt visible from his brow to his belt.

I speak of what I know. Though my drug is food, not drugs. And I continue to wean myself from processed foods to whole foods.

But the situation is unwinnable for users of hard drugs. The situation persists to the detriment of many. And the culture[22] of Wall

---

21 "10.8 Million Full-Time Workers Have a Substance Use Disorder." *The NSDUH Report*, 7 August 2014, www.samhsa.gov/data/sites/default/files/NSDUH-SP132-FullTime-2014/NSDUH-SP132-FullTime-2014.pdf

22 MSNBC. (2014, October 30). *Strippers & Drugs: Wall Street in the 1980s* [Video]. YouTube. https://youtu.be/-uVNtSnDnCA

Street and the portrayal of Wall Street in popular culture[23] even leads to possible destitution or death for some.

As to the culture of Wall Street and misconduct on Wall Street—drug abuse is a problem. I would not defend this culture, so I would also not dispute that this culture begets misconduct.

This expresses my informed opinion of Wall Street. Whatever differs from this, to the extent that the difference is negative, is indefensible. As this book is the summation of my case for something, with each Chapter an argument from evidence on behalf of many things—including the dangers of uncertainty, on the one hand, and certitude about danger, on the other—this book is a body of evidence.

The evidence is substantial, not selective. And this book is an argument about the necessity of proof.

The proof is in the sources, various and voluminous, upon which my case rests.

The case is in every page of this book.

*

"The events in our lives happen in a sequence in time, but in their significance to ourselves they find their own order, a timetable not necessarily—perhaps not possibly—chronological. The time as we know it subjectively is often the chronology that stories and novels follow: it is the continuous thread of revelation."

—Eudora Welty, *On Writing*

---

23 *The Wolf of Wall Street*. Directed by Martin Scorsese, performances by Leonardo DiCaprio and Matthew McConaughey, Paramount Pictures, 2013. YouTube, uploaded by Paramount Pictures, 24 December 2013 https://youtu.be/oz4TO7YxQRc

In writing this section last and reserving my final words for the end of the beginning, I see how the stories in this book have a sequence.

The stories refer to events, some of them ongoing, in which certain numbers—numbers pertaining to costs, from lives lost to COVID-19 to increases in the cost of living—are worse than before.

The numbers add context to the stories, because I care as much about the soundness of the numbers I cite—and the credibility of the sources I include—as I do about the sound of my voice on the page.

I care about the authenticity of my voice—that the sound is my own—more than whether everyone likes how I sound.

Whether the voice is sound and the sound different, whether the sound registers as a choice and echoes because the message is different, whether my voice gives voice to a conversation about insurance and investing—that is for readers to decide.

The facts speak for themselves.

CHAPTER 1
Toxic Assets

> **"'In order to remain undead, I must steal the life force of someone whose fate matters less to me than my own.' I've always supposed that Wall Street traders utter essentially the same sentence."**
>
> —Thomas C. Foster,
> *How to Read Literature Like a Professor*

I should be dead.

Obese and diabetic, I was a workaholic, toxic asset. But then, to improve and elongate my life, I disembarked from the diabetes train with a gastric bypass stop at the Cleveland Clinic.

Not the life I led up north, but the sun-drenched life I am living today in Florida—the life I want to keep living—far from the constant chase for money.

The chase runs beyond the Financial District of Manhattan in New York City. The chase traverses the world, crisscrossing the globe faster than the fastest rocket, replacing comprehension with computation and language with light.

The light distributes trillions to billions, according to algorithms that trade securities in silence. Upon these trades, currencies rise or fall, exports flow or imports flounder, and prices peak or markets plummet. Upon these trades, reason yields to reality. For the outcome of any single trade or series of trades can be irrational but real. No, the outcome *is* real—regardless of the dictates of reason or the laws of logic.

Upon this fact—and it is a fact—irrational outcomes occur all the time. And acceptance of this fact is the exception that proves the rule. Because attempts to outlast time, to beat the clock, are a waste.

An American investor can be down in the best of times or up during the hardest time. They can weather the stress of a personal storm or defy a storm of dust and destruction. An investor can lose his gains over time or protect his gains from the randomness of time. An investor can be right some of the time or a lot of the time, but not all the time.

The more an investor is right, the less time he devotes to the possibility—the probability—that his latest investment may go wrong. Success is not, after all, a source of humility.

Rare is the investor who is stoic, neither flamboyant in victory nor fatalistic in defeat. Rare is the investor who is a realist, neither an egotist in public nor an egomaniac in private. And rarest of all is the investor who is a skeptic, neither categorical in his answers nor contentious in his assertions.

Because it is easy to believe extraordinary claims without extraordinary evidence, fraudsters know how easy it is to fool investors. We fool ourselves all the time, especially when we conflate greatness with godliness. We quote a president as if he were a prophet, quote words that sound prophetic without questioning the origins of a quote, and fail to confirm whether the quote is true or the attribution sound.

Thus, we continue to attribute words about the people to a believer in government of the people, despite the absence of primary sources from the people. No doubt "Honest Abe" would appreciate the irony of the situation, given his famed quote[24]: "You can fool all the people some of the time and some of the people all the time, but you cannot fool all the people all the time."

About fooling yourself, do not doubt the truth of this quote[25]: "The first principle is that you must not fool yourself—and you are the easiest person to fool."

The quote is from Richard Feynman's[26] 1974 Caltech commencement address. In speaking to his fellow scientists about a fellowship of scientific integrity, Feynman speaks to the power

---

24 Parker, David B. "You Can Fool All the People: Did Lincoln Say It?" *History News Network*, 14 February 2016, www.historynewsnetwork.org/article/161924

25 Feynman, Richard. "Cargo Cult Science." *Caltech*, 14 June 1974, https://calteches.library.caltech.edu/51/2/CargoCult.pdf

26 Ibid.

of truth. He spoke truth to the powerful too, reminding them that the truth will out, that failure to tell the whole truth will out a popularizer of half-truths, that failure to tell nothing but the truth will out a purveyor of mistruths.

Feynman's quote should give investors pause, as some things are too unbelievable to sustain the willing suspension of disbelief.

Woe to the investor who believes he can divine the outcome of an investment as if he were the god of the trading machine. As if he were a machine-made man-god bursting with light.

Do not let the light blind or burn you. That light is a warning light—one that attracts the proud, the vain, and the envious.

That light also makes the truth visible.

*

> **"See, your murderers come with smiles. They come as your friends, the people who have cared for you all of your life, and they always seem to come at a time when you're at your weakest and most in need of their help."**
>
> —Henry Hill (Ray Liotta), *Goodfellas*

If we take Hill's statement as a fashion statement, the Wall Street version of this friend came with the best wardrobe and credentials. He came dressed befitting a man with addresses in Manhattan, Montauk, and Palm Beach. He came as a philanthropist, a power broker, and a patron of the arts. He came as the chairman of Nasdaq, the second-largest stock market in the world.

He came to steal.

He stole $18 billion[27] (or as much as $65 billion, including fictional profits) from banks, pension funds, charities, universities, and individual investors.

His name was Bernie Madoff.

Harry Markopolos asked the right questions. But those questions (in 2000, 2001, and 2005) were ignored by the U.S. Securities and Exchange Commission (SEC). But for the SEC's record of his requests, we would not know about his attempts to alert the authorities. And we would not know about his efforts to warn Wall Street and investors throughout the world about Madoff's crimes.

Markopolos's book, *No One Would Listen: A True Financial Thriller*[28], is true to its title. No one listened then for the same reason no one listens now (present company notwithstanding). Because reason—the marshaling of evidence in defense of an assertion—yields to the forces of arrogance and greed.

---

27 Peterson-Withorn, Chase. "The Investors Who Had To Pay Back Billions In Ill-Gotten Gains From Bernie Madoff's Ponzi Scheme." *Forbes*, 14 April 2021, www.forbes.com/sites/chasewithorn/2021/04/14/the-investors-who-had-to-pay-back-billions-in-ill-gotten-gains-from-bernie-madoffs-ponzi-scheme/

28 Markopolos, Harry. (2010). *No One Would Listen: A True Financial Thriller.* Wiley. www.wiley.com/en-gb/No+One+Would+Listen%3A+A+True+Financial+Thriller-p-9780470625767

No one wants to listen to the immutable logic of reality, especially when the fantasy of virtual reality is a beautiful symphony of trust. The hard reality of truth is a jangling discord of banging gavels, of judges demanding order and auctioneers finalizing orders.

The gavels resound from houses of justice to auction houses. There, the wronged seek recompense and sellers receive compensation. The victims of a con artist seek restitution and an institution loses works of art.

My alma mater, Brandeis University, is an institution betrayed by Madoff. His crimes betrayed the letter and spirit of the motto of my alma mater: "Truth even unto its innermost parts." His crimes betrayed the best of social and industrial remedies, blocking the disinfectant of sunlight and the policeman of electric light. And they insulted the memory of the people's lawyer, Louis Brandeis.

Madoff's crimes almost turned a museum, the Rose Art Museum[29] at Brandeis, into a mausoleum. His crimes almost cast the entire museum—the lights, tubes, lamps, sculptures, and paintings—into darkness.

The walls were to be effaced of history, rendering unto collectors the collection of a lifetime. The walls would have lain bare—stripped of pieces by Picasso, Lichtenstein, de Kooning, Warhol, Johns, Serra, and Sherman.

Alumni saved the art inside the museum but lost the Upper East Side's Brandeis House, a work of art far outside the museum and within walking distance of the best museums in New York City.

---

[29] "Brandeis University Considers Closing Rose Museum Due to Losses From Madoff Investments." *Art Observed*, 31 January 2009, www.artobserved.com/2009/01/brandeis-university-considers-closing-rose-museum-due-to-losses-from-madoff-investments/

Alumni lost a mansion of a house, owned by the son of the grandson of the Commodore, namesake of the university whose athletes are the Commodores of Vanderbilt University. Alumni lost Brandeis House[30], where Anderson Cooper's mother, Gloria Vanderbilt, once lived. Alumni lost their house, and two consecutive presidents of Brandeis lost their jobs, leaving the university with no claim to the title of the book about its own history.

The university of *A Host at Last*[31] was now a guest—a dues-paying member—in someone else's house. Alumni lost a one-off, either because the university needed money or because the president of the university needed to raise money.

Either way, the problem with any such sale—be it a plan to sell art or the sale of architecture—is that what sells for a small fortune can cost a large fortune to purchase a second time.

Imagine the loss of such a thing. Imagine the cost of losing so much, while trying to convince an investor that his wealth on paper is the equivalent of funny money—that, in fact, he has no money. And imagine trying to tell an investor that his wins are another investor's losses, and that all investors in the same fund are victims of fraud by the same fraudulent investment adviser.

Though it may be hard to imagine, it is not hard for a fraudster to commit such crimes. Take, for instance, charges that a CEO committed them. And more, that she fooled investors, retailers, reporters, and her own board of directors.

---

30 Moses, Claire. "Brandeis University sells UES alumni house for $32M." *The Real Deal*, 23 February 2015, www.therealdeal.com/2015/02/23/brandeis-university-sells-ues-alumni-house-for-32m/

31 Sachar, Abram L. (1995). *Brandeis University: A Host at Last*. Brandeis University Press. https://search.library.brandeis.edu/discovery/delivery/01BRAND_INST:BRAND/12411787470001921

Imagine she produced a machine that served to maintain the illusion of success, such that everything—from her style of dress to her speaking style—was part of her mirage.

Such was the case of Elizabeth Holmes[32], founder and CEO of Theranos. In addition to defrauding $144 million from three investors, she was also convicted of conspiracy to commit mail fraud.

The point about Madoff and Holmes is that Feynman's quote about truth—that the truth will out—does not account for time.

But justice takes time. We see this between the nature of the universe and the arc of the moral universe. We see it between the physics of Feynman's career and the metaphysics of a King's[33] campaign for freedom, or with Martin Luther King Jr.'s march through rain and the fire of a sweltering sun.

If too much time passes, justice becomes like time itself: relative. And relativism breeds injustice, which is why I refuse to be an accomplice to the fast undoing of common sense.

I have clients to help, not time to waste.

I also have a duty to remember and a right to disclose my encounter with the unjust, recalling the air of insecurity—the atmosphere of vulnerability—amidst the New York Society of Securities Analysts, aboard the physical security of the USS *Intrepid*. There, on the flight deck of *Intrepid*, with more than a dozen aircraft to my left—with my back to the Hudson and

---

32 Temme, Laura. "Jury Finds Theranos Founder Elizabeth Holmes Guilty on Four of Eleven Criminal Charges." *FindLaw*, 7 January 2022, www.findlaw.com/legalblogs/technologist/jury-finds-theranos-founder-elizabeth-holmes-guilty-on-four-of-eleven-criminal-charges/

33 84471k. (2010, June 13). *How Long? Not Long.. Martin Luther King* [Video]. YouTube. https://youtu.be/A22IMJNzRsM

Hell's Kitchen on the horizon—one of Madoff's colleagues tried to recruit me.

This person worked for Madoff's sons, Mark and Andrew Madoff. He did not work for their father, whose iniquities hampered his children, striking Mark with shame and killing him by suicide, while marking Andrew with cancer and leaving him to die alone.

As a coda to this story—a story that will not end until Madoff's name ends, until losses written in red end with payments rendered in blood, until the last debt Madoff's estate owes ends—Madoff's sister, Sondra Wiener[34], is now dead. The 87-year-old and her 90-year-old husband, Marvin, died in a suicide pact, three days after Valentine's Day 2022.

I do not look forward to reading another story about the family of Bernard Madoff. Not when I know how hard it is to look back and write about such a story. Nor do I welcome this reckoning of genealogy in which death pays off the arrears of the past and makes amends for the crimes of a dead man.

*

> **"People aren't that complicated, Joe. Good people, bad people. They generally look like what they are."**
>
> —Jimmy Dell (Steve Martin) to Joe Ross (Campbell Scott), *The Spanish Prisoner*

Dell's advice belongs to esteemed playwright, director, and author David Mamet.

---

[34] Ashford, Ben. "'They wanted to leave the world together': Bernie Madoff's elderly sister and her terminally ill husband died in 'suicide pact' in their Florida home." *Daily Mail*, 21 February 2022, www.dailymail.co.uk/news/article-10536589/Bernie-Madoffs-elderly-sister-husband-died-suicide-pact-terminally-ill.html

The voice defines how Mamet's characters speak. It creates a style—a rhythm—known as Mamet Speak: a pathological emphasis on semantics[35].

The harmony of words, like the major and minor scales of tonality, is the sound of confidence. And this is how Mamet's characters talk and how they make their marks feel.

The con artist imbues his mark with the confidence to suspend disbelief. This is the case when we hear Mamet resurrect Melville's *The Confidence-Man*, his modern retelling of that tale set on April Fool's Day.

Where Melville has discourse flow like the river on which the steamboat sails—the words rolling on a Mississippi of discursive passages and divergent paths, the passengers coming and going in a flood of benignity and betrayal—Mamet is more direct. He goes from life on the Mississippi, a pilot aboard the bridge, to piloting the dropping of F-bombs with speed and precision. He returns to water, mixing the patois of the boiler room with the patter of rain. He rattles the downpour with a deluge of abuse, arming his mouthpiece[36] with a set of steak knives and a pair of brass balls, all while telling a trio of salesmen to "fuck or walk."

Foul-mouthed though he is, and however fond of acronyms he may be, Blake (Alec Baldwin) is Mamet's sleaze of a motivational speaker in *Glengarry Glen Ross*. He looks like what he is: a con artist with a repertoire and a collection of props.

Blake flashes gold, handing his watch, a Rolex Day-Date, to Dave Moss (Ed Harris). Moss is a salesman whose name suits

---

[35] Freedman, Samuel G. "The Gritty Eloquence of David Mamet." *New York Times Magazine*, 21 April 1985, www.nytimes.com/1985/04/21/magazine/the-gritty-eloquence-of-david-mamet.html

[36] *Glengarry Glen Ross*. Directed by James Foley, performances by Alec Baldwin, Jack Lemmon, and Ed Harris, New Line Cinema, 1992. YouTube, uploaded by Reid Crandall, 31 October 2013 https://youtu.be/bkjfZctGMq8

the weather and whose suit—cheap, wet, and gray—speaks to his failure as a salesman.

Blake humiliates Moss with success. He informs Moss that the watch costs more than his car. He tells all the salesmen in the room that he, Blake, drives an $80,000 BMW. He says that he can go out there tonight, in the rain, with the same materials they have and make $15,000. And the coup de grâce is something they can see (from a distance) but not hold: a stack of salmon pink index cards—the Glengarry leads—tied together with gold.

To the salesmen, those leads are gold.

"And you don't get them," Blake says. "Why? Because to give them to you is just throwing them away. They're for closers."

And so, the scene begins and ends not as a mission of mercy but as a public service message. The message is a warning sign, because the pressure a salesman faces—the pressure he feels to close—should never obligate a consumer to buy anything.

Whether at street level or in the highest suite on Wall Street, the pressure to sell is constant, and it induces compliance without consent. Because what the adviser knows or the analyst feels is a force more intense than the highest pressure at the lowest depths of the seas and oceans. The pressure beneath the surface—hydrostatic pressure—can kill a man, while the pressure on Wall Street can destroy a man's soul.

The pressure to sell requires that a rarity in many places be a scarcity in most places on Wall Street.

The pressure to forsake conscience for commerce is commonplace on Wall Street.

*

> **"A policy of life insurance is the cheapest and safest mode of making a certain provision for one's family."**
>
> —Benjamin Franklin

Before founding the first university in the United States, and two decades before co-founding the United States itself, Benjamin Franklin founded an insurance company[37].

Before he signed the Declaration of Independence, the Constitution, the Treaty of Alliance with France, and the Treaty of Paris establishing peace with Great Britain, Franklin signed the Philadelphia Contributionship for the Insurance of Houses from Loss by Fire. This was the first property insurance company in the United States.

What Franklin valued as a form of protection, the law now recognizes as a form of property[38]. What we should value is what insurance (in this case, life insurance) can do: protect the existing value of an asset.

Put another way—the principle of buying insurance is to protect principal.

Protection is the answer to the one question few investors ask, and which most investment advisers do not volunteer to answer. That question is: What can you guarantee?

An adviser can guarantee two things. He can guarantee his commission—that he will receive one if you do business with him. And he can guarantee that what you buy *has no guarantee*. You may make money, lose money, or lose all your money.

---

37 "About Us." *The Philadelphia Contributionship*, www.1752.com/about-us/history

38 *Grigsby v. Russell*, 222 U.S. 149 (1911). www.supreme.justia.com/cases/federal/us/222/149/

In contrast, life insurance can protect your principal while providing tax-free income. The benefits, which I detail in subsequent chapters, are the basis of this book.

The benefits are many, measurable, and meaningful.

CHAPTER 2
A Bevy of Black Swans

"Wall Street never changes. The pockets change, the stocks change, but Wall Street never changes, because human nature never changes."
—Jesse Livermore, *How to Trade in Stocks*

Starting on election night in November 2000, for thirty six days, no one knows who will succeed the 42nd president of the United States. Then, nine days before the 43rd president's eighth month in office, America suffers the worst attack since Pearl Harbor.

Seven years and fifty-four days later, with the country at war and the economy in the worst recession since the Great Depression, the 44th president breaks the color barrier. The president wins reelection, confident that a member of his own party—a woman—will break the glass ceiling. She wins the popular vote but loses the 2016 election.

The 45th president is a real estate developer and TV host. Congress impeaches him twice.

Before the end of his second trial and acquittal, the COVID-19 pandemic kills 400,000 Americans. States go into lockdown, schools close, businesses fail, and riots ensue.

Fourteen days before the 46th president takes the oath of office, protesters storm the U.S. Capitol.

195 days later, on July 20, 2021, the world's richest man leaves Earth.

Seven months and five days later, on February 24, 2022, Russia invades Ukraine.

Eighty-one days later, on May 16, 2022, oil prices hit $114 a barrel. The next day, the U.S. officially surpasses one million COVID-19 deaths.

Between the end of spring and the first week of fall, bank failures and mortgage boycotts occur throughout China. The yuan then hits an all-time low.

Two weeks before Thanksgiving, the third-largest cryptocurrency exchange files for bankruptcy.

One month later, a special committee of the House of Representatives approves criminal referrals against the 45th president.

*

"We humans are the victims of an asymmetry in the perception of random events. We attribute our successes to our skills, and our failures to external events outside our control, namely to randomness."

—Nassim Nicholas Taleb, *The Black Swan: The Impact of the Highly Improbable*

Black swan events are not new, as Black Thursday (October 24, 1929) and Black Tuesday (October 29, 1929) demonstrate.

The events marked the end of easy credit, revoking the nation's moral credit while charging creditors with the power to repossess all goods past due.

The reckoning came in "black blizzards" of dirt, culminating on a Black Sunday[39] of dust, which delivered men to the ground

---

[39] Greenspan, Jesse. "What Happened on Black Sunday?" *History.com*, 14 April 2015, www.history.com/news/remembering-black-sunday

from which they were taken. Dust they were, and to dust they returned. The reckoning was a foretaste of soil and blood, as the worst hard time of nature preceded the worst times and hardships caused by human nature.

The whirlwind came in wars hot and cold, with the near annihilation of a people and the power to annihilate the world. Abhorrent though these events were, they were no aberration. And they should not surprise us given the evil that men do and the fallenness of man.

After the century of total war—from the self-deception of the Great War to the end of the Second World War, from the use of poison gas on the Western Front to genocide and gassing operations on the Eastern Front—the first great shock of the twenty-first century should not surprise us. The path to 9/11 is long and clear.

In fact, the path is anything but improbable. We see it when looking back on the first World Trade Center bombing, from watching TV news coverage of the 1993 attack to living in New York City on September 11, 2001. We see it from the distance of the screen to the immediacy of the scene, able to feel but not fully articulate the scented past of death.

In examining Osama bin Laden's declaration of jihad against Americans[40], the bombings of our embassies in East Africa, and the attack on the USS Cole, 9/11 looks like what it is: a day of fire after years of warning.

---

40 "Osama bin Laden's Declaration of Jihad Against Americans." *9/11 Memorial & Museum*, www.911memorial.org/sites/default/files/inline-files/1996%20Osama%20bin%20Laden%27s%201996%20Fatwa%20against%20United%20States_0.pdf

Looking back over a thousand months in a hundred years, one fire is remarkable: that from Little Boy. As the son of man's power to harness the sun, Little Boy still burns.

Despite leaflets warning of devastation, and despite explicit warnings of the devastating power of America's newest weapon, death came from the ash of stars[41] that had lived and died long before the oldest mountains of the moon were born.

Thus does history record the atomic bombing of Hiroshima.

The point is, we are not spectators to history. We ride the currents of events, enduring the rapids and avoiding (hopefully) the shoals, regardless of the stories we tell ourselves to live.

Many of the economic stories we tell ourselves are like those that politicians, reporters, and economists tell themselves. The endings are clear and clearly incompatible, with the most

---

[41] Pellegrino, Charles. (2010). *The Last Train from Hiroshima: The Survivors Look Back*. Henry Holt and Company. www.biblio.com/book/last-train-hiroshima-survivors-look-back/d/894880258

famous economist[42] saying, "In the long run we are all dead," and the most famous investor[43] saying, "Over the long term, the stock market news will be good."

Never mind that the long run is independent of time while the long term is a product of time. Because the two lack specificity, the phrases mean different things to different people. And about the men who said these things—about an aphorism by John Maynard Keynes versus the aphoristic stylings of Warren Buffett—it should be said that death is certain while good news about the stock market is not a certainty.

And Buffett, the Oracle of Omaha, does not specify how long the long term is.

Were he to say what the long term is—and were he to abide by what he says—we could test the accuracy of his assertion. But because he implies that clock-time is more important than event-time, that stock market news will be better than events in the news, his assertion is incomplete. Because he does not define the terms of experiment, his assertion about the long term is meaningless. And so, Buffett can never be wrong. But he can also never be right, so long as his assertion is ambiguous.

Buffett can afford to be wrong. But most investors cannot afford to bet that Buffett is right.

As an investor, I would rather know the stakes than stake my lot on the unknown. As I do not like to gamble, I would rather be smart than look shrewd. And because I do not like to lose, I

---

[42] Evans, David. "How long is the long run?" *World Bank Blogs*, 11 April 2018,

[43] Holodny, Elena. "Warren Buffett's Vision for the Stock Market in 100 Years? A $1 Million Dow." *Inc.*, 21 September 2017, www.inc.com/business-insider/warren-buffett-dow-go-over-1-million-100-years.html

insist on understanding the rules before I sign a contract or write a check.

Put in the starkest terms, rules can be a dialogue in precision—a colloquy between good and evil. A person's fate can hinge on a coin toss. He or she can stand to win everything without knowing or being told what he stands to lose.

Take the scene in the film *No Country for Old Men*[44], for instance, where the proprietor of a gas station bargains with Death. That the proprietor almost loses his life proves the value of knowing *all* the facts in advance. Serving as a metaphor for time, the scene uses timing belts to outline the proprietor's head, tightening a row of nooses around his neck. These nooses frame the shot, suggesting that no place is too far—no country too foreign—to escape time. Even a star on a signpost, like a badge on the frontier, cannot stop time. And this Texaco station of a would-be sheriff's station, windswept on the outside and worn on the inside, cannot reverse time.

What follows is an exercise in exactitude between the proprietor and the killer Anton Chigurh (Javier Bardem).

INT. GAS STATION/GROCERY - DAY

CHIGURH
... What's the most you've ever lost
on a coin toss?

PROPRIETOR
Sir?

---

[44] *No Country for Old Men*. Directed by Joel Coen and Ethan Coen, performances by Jarvier Bardem and Gene Jones, Miramax Films, 2007. YouTube, uploaded by Miramax, 26 November 2014 https://youtu.be/opbi7d42s8E

CHIGURH
The most. You ever lost. On a coin toss.

PROPRIETOR
I don't know. I couldn't say.

Chigurh is digging in his pocket. A quarter: he tosses it. He slaps it onto his forearm but keeps it covered.

CHIGURH
Call it.

PROPRIETOR
Call it?

CHIGURH
Yes.

PROPRIETOR
For what?

CHIGURH
Just call it.

PROPRIETOR
Well—we need to know what it is we're callin' for here.

CHIGURH
You need to call it. I can't call it for you. It wouldn't be fair. It wouldn't even be right.

PROPRIETOR
I didn't put nothin' up.

CHIGURH

Yes you did. You been putting it up your whole life. You just didn't know it. You know what date is on this coin?

PROPRIETOR

No.

CHIGURH

Nineteen fifty-eight. It's been traveling twenty-two years to get here. And now it's here. And it's either heads or tails, and you have to say. Call it.

A long beat.

PROPRIETOR

Look ... I got to know what I stand to win.

CHIGURH

Everything.

PROPRIETOR

How's that?

CHIGURH

You stand to win everything. Call it.

PROPRIETOR

All right. Heads then.

*

"The stakes are immense, the task colossal, the time is short. But we may hope—we must hope—that man's own creation, man's own genius, will not destroy him."

—Albert Einstein

If you do not know what you stand to lose, or you do not know to ask what may happen if you lose, you stand to lose everything. And if all voices talk about winning while the few who know say nothing, you may lose everything.

Consider the context in which I write these words. Today marks twenty-five days after the twentieth anniversary of 9/11. It is fifty-two days from a Chinese anniversary like no other, commemorating two decades of U.S. involvement in Afghanistan, concluding in a rout by the Taliban and bellicose rhetoric from China.

These events have many causes. Chief among them is the failure—the colossal failure—of people with the intelligence to know the truth to study or speak the truth. More than a loss of $2.26 trillion[45], these events represent an irrevocable loss of men and materiel.

[45] Rahman, Khaleda. "How Much Did the War in Afghanistan Cost?" *Newsweek*, 16 August 2021 www.newsweek.com/how-much-did-war-afghanistan-cost-1619687

Numbers cannot summarize the significance of our loss. Nothing we say or do can reverse the reality of our loss, because the world will long remember how we lost.

We cannot forget the images of our loss, from the day the war began, when the 43rd president said peace and freedom would prevail, to the day the war ended, when the 46th president said we cannot afford to win.

What began with hubris ended in humiliation, marking a new and unsettling beginning for America and her allies throughout the world.

What, you ask, does military security have to do with financial or retirement security? I can answer in one word: everything.

Everything we hope to preserve and protect depends on the accuracy of the information we have. For we cannot make an informed decision if we cannot decide what is true. We are mere witnesses to a generation, a lost generation, born of two decades of misinformation from institutions of little or no social and political capital.

The White House, the Pentagon, Congress, the media, the CIA—all these institutions bear responsibility for the gross misallocation of resources, resulting in claims devoid of proof, policies of insufficient proof, and the elimination of the burden of proof.

If you seek a monument to this era, look at the monuments in memory of the dead. Look at the emblems of service and faith, where Stars of David stand between crosses, row on row, and where headstones include the star and crescent, where valor proudly sleeps.

Look at the cost of defense on behalf of the good versus spending on civilian goods. Look at the guns versus butter model of macroeconomics.

The two models are as one, piling together debts we cannot honor with debts that dishonor the freedom of all Americans who serve and save.

The two models compete for and consume the same resources, causing the economy to stagnate and prices to rise, the result of which is stagflation.

The stagflation of the 1970s is not the potential stagflation of the 2020s, though the conditions—a simultaneous shock in the supply of goods and the money supply—are similar.

At the time of writing—in the aftermath of lockdowns and the closure of businesses due to COVID-19, along with the end of a federal moratorium on evictions and with 3.5 million[46] households at risk of losing their homes—the shocks come as waves of increasing might, not as aftershocks of lower intensity.

The shocks include yearlong rises in rental prices (11.4 percent[47]) and the price of gasoline (41.8 percent[48]). On top of that, there's a 12 percent[49] expansion of the money supply.

Economists disagree about how to address these shocks.

---

46 Ivanova, Irina. "With eviction moratorium gone, 3.5 million U.S. households could lose their home, Goldman Sachs estimates." *CBS News*, 2 September 2021, www.cbsnews.com/news/eviction-moratorium-ends-families-risk-losing-homes-analysis/

47 Domm, Patti. "Inflation was hot in July, but rent isn't showing up yet and could drive prices higher." *CNBC*, 11 August 2021, www.cnbc.com/2021/08/11/inflation-rent-could-be-a-persistent-factor-in-higher-consumer-prices.html

48 "Gasoline Inflation in the United States (1968-2022)." *U.S. Inflation Calculator*, www.usinflationcalculator.com/inflation/gasoline-inflation-in-the-united-states/

49 Brettell, Karen. "Analysis: Economists eye surging money supply as inflation fears mount." *Reuters*, 17 June 2021, www.reuters.com/business/economists-eye-surging-money-supply-inflation-fears-mount-2021-06-17/

Looking back on a losing strategy of WIN[50] (Whip Inflation Now) and a no-win situation for most politicians, the policies to roll back stagflation were as controversial as America's policy of rollback. The focus on victory—of reducing the money supply while increasing the supply of arms, of withstanding temporary pain for long-term gains in the financial markets—were the respective and joint policies of Paul Volcker and Ronald Reagan.

The policies proved that this country would pay the price to defeat the thief of inflation and the threat of military conflagration. And the chairman of the Federal Reserve and the president of the United States would together bear the burden.

The policies cost the president twenty-six House seats in the 1982 midterm elections. This was but a small price for the promise of a huge victory in 1984. He won reelection to the White House while simultaneously winning the war (without firing a shot) against the apostles of *Nineteen Eighty-Four*.

Consider, too, the irony of a Democrat (Volcker) working in concert with a president who was a former Democrat. And that Volcker,

---

[50] "Whip Inflation Now (WIN)." *Gerald R. Ford Presidential Library*, www.fordlibrarymuseum.gov/museum/artifactcollectionsamples/win.html

who was Jimmy Carter's best and most important appointee, was also working with Carter's successor.

But because no one could time the recovery brought about by Volcker's policies—except to say the time had come for the Fed to adopt his policies—the timing was too late to help Carter and not hurt Reagan. So the world's most powerful central banker could not time the economy, and the world's most powerful opponent of central planning could not time the political markets. The result was then that no investor could best the combined forces of the chairman of the Federal Reserve and the commander in chief.

To my earlier point about knowing versus doing, about agreeing to act versus acting itself, Volcker's policies were not new. He did not conjure success inside a two-story room, beneath a chandelier and beside a collection of globes and glass etchings. He was no sorcerer. He had no cauldron to heat or pot to stir. He had only a pump—a metaphorical device—to prime or plug.

Volcker did his job amidst record joblessness, while President Reagan watched his own job approval rating fall.

Thus did a theory of finance, reversion to the mean, meet a man with a theory of government.

Thus did Volcker stabilize the economy as Reagan reversed the mood of the country.

Thus did a precedent set by Carter[51], in a speech mourning a crisis of confidence among the American people, yield to a series of set pieces about "Morning in America."[52]

*

"We are the United States of Amnesia, we learn nothing because we remember nothing."

—Gore Vidal, *Imperial America: Reflections on the United States of Amnesia*

In 2022, as a result of the COVID-19 pandemic, inflation reached 8.5%, the highest rate since 1982. So, 78 million Americans now living—those born after the high inflation rates of the 1980s—have no memory of inflation. And when those born after the death of double-digit inflation experience inflation for the first time, I see one-quarter of a nation ill-prepared to deal with inflation.

Because inflation is at a forty-year high, and because members of the Federal Reserve disagree about what factors influence inflation, I see a central bank more at war with itself than with inflation.

---

51 reeece888888. (2012, May 2). *Jimmy Carter's Full 'Crisis of Confidence' Speech* [Video]. YouTube. https://youtu.be/kakFDUeoJKM

52 Museum of the Moving Image. (2016, June 10). *Prouder, Stronger, Better* [Video]. YouTube. https://youtu.be/m_B2gZCB85c

Fed chairman Jerome Powell[53] says, "Inflation expectations are terribly important." But Jeremy Rudd[54], a senior Fed economist, disagrees.

In fact, Rudd's paper on inflation challenges the neatness of economic theories. He counters expectations with evidence, or rather exposes the lack thereof, saying, "[This] apotheosis has occurred with minimal *direct* evidence, next-to-no examination of alternatives that might do a similar job fitting the available facts, and zero introspection as to whether it makes sense to use the particular assumptions or derived implications of a theoretical model."

How, then, can economists check inflation if they do not change their approach to inflation? How can they insist they are right when the evidence proves they are wrong?

*

"Nobody knows anything ... Not one person in the entire motion picture field knows for a certainty what's going to work. Every time out it's a guess and, if you're lucky, an educated one."

—William Goldman, *Adventures in the Screen Trade*

What everybody should know is that the soundness of a comment or the certainty of a claim is a matter of evidence. What a person can show matters most. After all, evidence is more credible than a show of emotion.

---

53 Chappatta, Brian. "Fed's Infighting Shows It Lacks Answers About Inflation." *Bloomberg*, 28 September 2021, https://www.bloomberg.com/opinion/articles/2021-09-28/federal-reserve-s-infighting-shows-it-lacks-answers-about-inflation

54 Rudd, Jeremy B. (2021). "Why Do We Think That Inflation Expectations Matter for Inflation? (And Should We?)," Finance and Economics Discussion Series 2021-062. Washington: Board of Governors of the Federal Reserve System, https://doi.org/10.17016/FEDS.2021.062

Because of this standard—because we *have* standards—we can show that many know so little about so much.

In rereading predictions about a future that never was, the truth of Goldman's maxim shows how wrong the experts were about everything. In fact, the experts were "not even wrong." Their theories were so incomplete as to be irrelevant.

Statements about the economic decline and fall of the United States were impossible to prove because they were impossible to know in advance. Not that this fact—that the experts *had no facts*—deterred them from profiting by prophesying about the financial eclipse of America by Japan.

The predictions say more about the economics of issuing predictions than the care necessary to check the legitimacy of certain economic predictions.

In so many words, doom was then and is now a boon for publishers.

Near the end of the 1980s, the best-selling predictions of America's future were those of imminent war. We foresaw the invasion of the United States by the Empire of Japan. We foresaw an economic Pearl Harbor of sorts, and a final victory for the Japanese forces.

The predictions were yellow with cowardice, or a "yellow peril" for the Information Age. They turned a Norway spruce at Rockefeller Center into the tallest bonsai tree at Hirohito Center. They turned Christian soldiers into slaves of the Chrysanthemum Throne and a Christmas yet to come into the Ghost of Christmas Yet to Come.

A particular apparition[55] even warned Americans to stop buying Japanese cars. Times were dire.

The warning was also a wrong done to a people, the Japanese people, by persons purporting to speak for the American people. The warning was an infamy of hatred and deceit, about Christmas Day 2001.

Imagine a few years from now. It's December, and the whole family's going to see the big Christmas tree in Hirohito Center. Go ahead, keep buying Japanese cars.

Imagine presenting those words to a group of Pontiac dealers in the New York metropolitan area. Imagine the dealers agreeing to air those words, which they did. Imagine, too, the response from the head of advertising for General Motors (GM), makers of Pontiac.

That the response was a nonresponse is no surprise. A person cannot endow a corporation with reason and conscience. Nor can a person transform an article of fiction—the legal fiction of personhood—into an article of faith, because corporations are not human beings. Were the opposite true, corporations would answer to a higher law and humble themselves before the ultimate lawgiver.

Now, imagine the irony of what happened to Pontiac. Not one of the ten best-selling vehicles[56] in 2001 was a Pontiac. Seven of the ten were, however, American-made cars and trucks, with the Ford F-Series number one overall.

---

[55] The MacNeil/Lehrer NewsHour. Boston, MA: NewsHour Productions, American Archive of Public Broadcasting (GBH and the Library of Congress), Boston, MA and Washington, DC. Retrieved from http://americanarchive.org/catalog/cpb-aacip-507-0z70v8b596

[56] Riches, Erin. "Top 10 Best Selling Vehicles in 2001." *Edmunds*, 12 May 2009, www.edmunds.com/car-reviews/top-10/top-10-best-selling-vehicles-in-2001.html

The irony is tragic. The era in question represents the errors of groupthink. Few choose to put the question to a group of economists or politicians, so we may understand how fear—nameless, unreasoning, unjustified terror—makes it difficult for individuals to think.

Few imagined, after all, that the sun would set on the land of the rising sun. Few foresaw that exorbitant prices would do to the land what no disaster had done up to that point: crash Japan's economy without bombing her cities.

Few imagined that Japan's real estate bubble would burst, her industries decline, or that negative interest rates and negative population growth would make her older but not necessarily wiser. And few predicted wariness would haunt Japan, that China would come to taunt and threaten Japan, displacing her as the world's second largest economy, and that America would also rise.

Imagine if the experts had said or done nothing to embarrass themselves.

Perhaps it beggars the imagination to picture modesty in the face of malice, or to picture the faces of innocents betrayed and imprisoned by their own nation. But America's reaction to Japan is a study of overreaction toward all things Japanese.

Just in its prosecution of Japanese aggression, and charitable in its rebuilding of Japanese society after the Second World War, the United States was nonetheless unjust in its treatment of Japanese Americans during and after the war.

Not until February 19, 1976, thirty years to the day, did regret turn to resolution.

Not until the 40th vice president of the United States became the 38th commander in chief—never having won election to either office—did a Ford act like a Lincoln, renouncing the order issued by the only man to have won four presidential elections.

Not until we act according to Acts will we be unafraid.

Until then, let us be mindful of economists or politicians whose monetary policy would convert a base reaction into a base currency. Let us be wary of those who might cause us to trade our freedom for nothing but fear. And let us identify those who want us to live in a constant state of fear, where the year is 1984[57] and the time is 100 seconds to midnight[58], such that today is our last day and tomorrow is doomsday.

Add twenty seconds to the time remaining to give us 120 seconds, and then denounce Two Minutes Hate. Because if destruction be our lot—if we are to be the authors and finishers of our own demise—let us have nothing to do with a lynch party. And let us have nothing to do with the rally held outside the Capitol on July 1, 1987. Remember that on that day, David Keene of the American Conservative Union brandished a gold-tinted noose (the "Golden Rope Award"[59]) and accused the board of directors and chairman of Toshiba, and a supporting cast in the highest echelons of the Japanese government, of treachery.

Better for us to die for a noble lie than an ignoble act of hatred in which members of Congress smashed[60] a Toshiba radio with sledgehammers.

---

57 *1984*. Directed by Michael Redford, performances by John Hurt and Suzanna Hamilton, 20th Century Fox, 1984. YouTube, uploaded by Movieclips, 22 April 2015 https://youtu.be/XvGmOZ5T6_Y

58 Mecklin, John. "At doom's doorstep: It is 100 seconds to midnight." *Bulletin of the Atomic Scientists*, 20 January 2022, www.thebulletin.org/doomsday-clock/current-time/

59 Skidmore, Dave. "Rep. Bentley: 'None Dare Call It Toshiba.'" *Associated Press*, 2 July 1987, www.apnews.com/article/c5f3c744b7b368b7a83b895f43872afe

60 Congressional Archives Carl Albert Center. (2021, February 19). *James Jones on MacNeil/Lehrer Report—Toshiba Who Sold Sensitive Equipment to the Soviets* [Video]. YouTube. https://youtu.be/K0RHymZZY3Y

Best for us not to resort to methods of self-hypnosis, where turning the needle on a Toshiba radio or looking at the spindles on a cassette player weakens our resistance to the power of suggestion.

Best for us not to suggest that all U.S. politicians and lobbyists should look at the flag of the sun. And certainly when some would take the circle at the center and cut it out in little dots, marking their targets with an "S,"[61] before shouting, "It's a Sony" and then smashing every screen in sight.

In contrast, we may opt to adjust the contrast on a Sony TV and use the red oval from the Trinitron logo[62] as the red pill[63] of truth. In doing so, we would go from the detonation of the first nuclear bomb to the first demonstration of a breakthrough in TV technology.

We would go from the Trinity test[64] to the test card on a Trinitron TV[65].

We would go from isolating electrons to firing three beams from one electron gun.

We would go from 1945 to 1968, from ruin to resurrection, before reviewing U.S. relations with Japan during the 1980s.

Perhaps we would see better from more than six miles or six feet away—far from the afterglow of a weapon of war or the aftermath

---

61 It's a Sony Logo." (n.d.). Wikimedia Commons. Retrieved August 11, 2023, from https://commons.wikimedia.org/wiki/File:It%27s_a_Sony_Logo.png.

62 Wozniak, Marshall. "Trinitron." *Visions4 Magazine*, 8 May 2017, www.visions4netjournal.com/page-five-trinitron/

63 Wikipedia. (2023, August). Red pill and blue pill. In Wikipedia. URL: https://en.wikipedia.org/wiki/Red_pill_and_blue_pill

64 "Trinity Test—1945." *Atomic Heritage Foundation*, https://ahf.nuclearmuseum.org/ahf/history/trinity-test-1945/

65 Santo, Brian. "The Consumer Electronics Hall of Fame: Sony Trinitron." *IEEE Spectrum*, 20 December 2018, https://spectrum.ieee.org/the-consumer-electronics-hall-of-fame-sony-trinitron

of a trade war. Perhaps then we would have the knowledge that hindsight affords: that victory is ours. And perhaps it takes time to see past the green light, the light in the middle of the screen, before people realize that the light is a product of its time, not a product for time immemorial.

The product emits light and transmits snow regardless of the weather. Because the product is a box—a cabinet of wood and metal—without divine force or power.

The product is in fact a relic, not a reliquary of silver and gold. The product is a television set—an analog TV—with no market share in America.

With the exception of the Walkman, another Sony product, no other product symbolizes the decline and fall of "Japan Inc." like the analog TV. Both products are models of excellence in performance and elegance in design. But neither is relevant to how we live now, for we live in a digital world—a world of ones and zeros—with its own grammar. In this world, no article is necessary before Amazon, and the definite article "the" introduces the cloud. Where Seattle is the home of Amazon and server farms house the cloud. And where Apple Park has an apricot orchard and Apple is the world's most valuable company.

In this world, sixty-one[66] of the 100 most valuable companies are U.S. corporations. Only three are Japanese.

In this world, the most valuable automaker is Tesla and Tesla's CEO is one of the select few richest people in history.

---

[66] Press release. "US companies dominate the world's stock markets in 2021 – Switzerland has three corporations among the world's 100 most valuable companies." *EY*, 29 December 2021, www.ey.com/en_ch/news/2021/12/us-companies-dominate-the-worlds-stock-markets-in-2021-switzerland-has-three-corporations-among-the-worlds-100-most-valuable-companies

In this world, Elon Musk[67] is *Time*'s 2021 "Person of the Year."

*

"The curious task of economics is to demonstrate to men how little they really know about what they imagine they can design."

—F.A. Hayek, *The Fatal Conceit*

The intelligence to design is separate from the wisdom to discern. No one—not even the most successful forecaster—can know the future. Not that this fact deters people from trying to plan the course of industry and trade, or that people want to know the facts about Japan's Ministry of International Trade and Industry (MITI).

The end of MITI lies outside Japan, in a city where the truth is forbidden and a hero has no name.

The truth is in the image of a man in plainclothes, not a plainclothesman. For the image of Tank Man[68] is a picture of

[67] Ball et al. "2021 Person of the Year: Elon Musk." *Time*, 13 December 2021, www.time.com/person-of-the-year-2021-elon-musk/

[68] Tank Man (Tiananmen Square protester). (n.d.). [Photograph]. Retrieved August 11, 2023, from Wikipedia. https://en.wikipedia.org/wiki/Tank_Man#/media/File%3ATank_Man_(Tiananmen_Square_protester).jpg

spontaneity—a profile in courage—beyond the state's ability to plan or comprehend.

A martyr for democracy and a martyr to the Goddess of Democracy, Tank Man remains anonymous. And yet he lives despite efforts to deny his existence and despite the fact that he may no longer exist. He lives because images of him exist in the minds of freedom-loving peoples throughout the world.

His image is illegal to see or share in mainland China. It is a crime there—a thoughtcrime—to commemorate the Tiananmen Square Incident or condemn the Tiananmen Square Massacre.[69]

But the history of the June Fourth Incident, and of the incident involving Tank Man the next day, is the history of much more than the 1989 Democracy Movement.

The movement died with the cessation of movement among the protesters, when the People's Liberation Army (PLA) "liberated" Tiananmen Square of freedom. When, after crushing the largest icon of freedom, breaking it like bone by stamping their boots on the statue's body and face, with the Goddess of Democracy[70] lying in the streets, the PLA rid the streets of people and made Beijing safe for communism.

Not content to arrest or execute dissidents at home, Beijing also targeted dissidents abroad.

---

69 "Assignment: China—Tiananmen Square." *USC US-China Institute*, 31 May 2014, www.china.usc.edu/assignment-china-tiananmen-square

70 "Picture Show: 1989 Tiananmen Square Incident." *China Today*, www.chinatoday.com/history/tiananmen_1989/tiananmen_1989_19.htm

Subsequent and permanent protection may not have occurred if not for the Emergency Chinese Immigration Relief Act of 1989[71], which Congress passed and which President George H.W. Bush vetoed. Or if not for the House's vote (390-5) to override the veto and the White House's press conference the day before the Senate voted (62-37) to sustain the veto. Or if not for actions during and after the vote.

Had the president not issued Executive Order 12711[72]—or signed the Chinese Student Protection Act of 1992[73]—my alma mater would have suffered. Brandeis University would have lost a champion of truth. And Shen Tong[74], a student at a university named for the people's lawyer, would have been deported to the People's Republic of China.

Lost in the tumult, however, was the truth about plans[75] by representatives of the world's second largest economy to flee the world's most populous country. Yes, Japanese diplomats had plans—and two bicycles—to escape China.

---

[71] Kurlander, David. "'He Was Talking about an Executive Order': Nancy Pelosi and President George H.W. Bush's Battle Over China." *CAFE*, 13 August 2020, www.cafe.com/article/he-was-talking-about-an-executive-order-nancy-pelosi-and-president-george-h-w-bushs-battle-over-china/

[72] Peters, Gerhard and John T. Woolley. "Executive Order 12711—Policy Implementation With Respect to Nationals of the People's Republic of China." *The American Presidency Project*, www.presidency.ucsb.edu/documents/executive-order-12711-policy-implementation-with-respect-nationals-the-peoples-republic

[73] Chinese Student Protection Act of 1992, 8 U.S.C. 1255 note (1992). www.govinfo.gov/content/pkg/STATUTE-106/pdf/STATUTE-106-Pg1969.pdf

[74] Brandeis Alumni Association. "Shen Tong '91 on the Front Line Against Coronavirus." *Brandeis | Alumni, Friends and Family*, 19 April 2020, https://alumni.brandeis.edu/stories/alumni/front-lines/tong-shen.html

[75] Ryall, Julian. "Tiananmen Square: Japanese diplomats feared Chinese troops would storm embassy." *South China Morning Post*, 4 June 2019, www.scmp.com/news/asia/east-asia/article/3013041/tiananmen-square-japanese-diplomats-feared-chinese-troops-would

Lost in the tumult of politics was the continuation of politics by other means, of treasure without war, and of the creative destruction of technology and trade. Lost was the fact that Japan had already lost the future to China.

Not that Japanese or U.S. officials accepted this fact, or that either group knew it. In fact, both groups continued to believe that Japan owned the future. There was a belief that America was a sickly nation, and that the president of the United States was himself sick. This belief—that Americans were economically ill and that President Bush was physically ill—looked believable, particularly after Bush vomited[76] in Japanese Prime Minister Kiichi Miyazawa's lap.

The incident became a campaign issue during the 1992 U.S. presidential election, with Bill Clinton using Miyazawa's words against Bush.

About his refusal to feel Miyazawa's pain or applaud the prime minister's "sympathy"[77] for the United States, Clinton[78] said, in his acceptance speech at the Democratic National Convention, "When I am your president, the rest of the world will not look down on us with pity but up to this with respect again."

After he became president, Clinton's rhetoric went from bellicose to benign. Gone was his contempt for the "butchers of Beijing" and his broadsides against Japan.

---

76 George H. W. Bush vomiting incident. (n.d.). In Wikipedia. Retrieved August 11, 2023, from https://en.wikipedia.org/wiki/George_H._W._Bush_vomiting_incident

77 Reid, T.R. "Japan's Embattled Prime Minister Opens New Session of Parliament." *Washington Post*, 25 January 1992, www.washingtonpost.com/archive/politics/1992/01/25/japans-embattled-prime-minister-opens-new-session-of-parliament/e082c814-fedf-44b5-b67b-d08214438834/

78 "Bill Clinton 1992 Acceptance Speech." *C-SPAN*, 16 July 1992, www.c-span.org/video/?27166-1/bill-clinton-1992-acceptance-speech

Fifteen years after President Clinton left office, between the time Hillary Clinton ran for president and Donald Trump won the presidency, America still had the world's largest economy. And the coming war with Japan was a bust. It never happened. Meanwhile *The Coming War with Japan*[79] was a best seller in America and Japan.

We would be wise to remember the above, mindful of how unpredictable the future is.

*

"Almost all empires were created by force, but none can be sustained by it. Universal rule, to last, needs to translate force into obligation. Otherwise, the energies of the rulers will be exhausted in maintaining their dominance at the expense of their ability to shape the

[79] "The Coming War with Japan." *C-SPAN*, 30 April 1991, www.c-span.org/video/?18335-1/the-coming-war-japan

future, which is the ultimate task of statesmanship. Empires persist if repression gives way to consensus."

—Henry Kissinger, *On China*

Were we mindful of the cultural contradictions of Chinese state capitalism, that Beijing cannot indefinitely enrich and starve the people, that economic success cannot purchase political silence, we would know that the mind is essential to the life of a modern economy. And we would know that the worst thing China could do to itself is believe its own propaganda, and treat man as a machine, feeding him—fueling his material wants—while denying the existence of the immaterial power of his soul; that man is an individual, and Tank Man the personification of the will of the individual, which no system can crush; that no system can promote education but police thought, to the point where the workplace is a haven of creativity and the home a place free of reflection.

Eventually the machine breaks down.

When the machine is the state—and when Beijing relies on machines to surveil and sequester the people—the system is in trouble.

When the state locks down Shanghai[80], emptying the streets of all traffic save police dogs, China is in trouble. And when the dogs themselves are robots that bark orders, or when drones broadcast a soul-destroying message about the need for residents to stay inside, then the soul's desire for freedom is also controlled.

The past repeats itself. This is evident when the party responsible for the Great Leap Forward takes another leap backward. It is evident in the form of zero-COVID restrictions and political violence. It is evident when the Chinese Communist Party (CCP)

---

[80] Landen, Xander. "Shanghai Residents Scream From Windows, Get Drone Lockdown Warning: Videos." *Newsweek*, 10 April 2022 www.newsweek.com/shanghai-residents-scream-windows-get-drone-lockdown-warning-videos-1696732

is party to famine and plague. And when it learns nothing from history because it censors history, the past becomes present.

The situation in China is impossible to ignore.

The situation puts the lie to the "China for a day"[81] dream of enlightened leadership. And it shows that engineers with political power are no more enlightened than career politicians who seek to reengineer society.

As for the "optics" of the situation, a word whose secondary meaning is of primary importance to politicians ... well, perceptions differ. What looks bad to us looks like the cost of doing business in China.

How we perceive the situation in China is less important to Xi Jinping—the president of the People's Republic of China—than the perception Xi conveys to the Chinese. The perception of absolute power is the reality of Xi's absolutism, where no one—not even the former premier of China—is safe from his policy of state control.

Fear is the currency of reality in China.

Fear purchases power at the expense of all other powers, which explains capital outflows[82] and plans by U.S. tech companies to shift production[83] out of China.

---

[81] Welch, Matt. "Thomas L. Friedman Wants Us 'to be China for a day,' to 'authorize the right solutions.'" *Reason*, 24 May 2010, www.reason.com/2010/05/24/thomas-l-friedman-wants-us-to/

[82] xLee, Amanda. "China's capital outflows hit US$8.8 billion in October amid 'notable shift' by foreign investors." *South China Morning Post*, 9 November 2022, www.scmp.com/economy/economic-indicators/article/3198998/chinas-capital-outflows-hit-us88-billion-october-amid-notable-shift-foreign-investors

[83] Wakabayashi, Daisuke and Tripp Mickle. "Tech Companies Slowly Shift Production Away From China." *New York Times*, 1 September 2022 www.nytimes.com/2022/09/01/business/tech-companies-china.html?smid=nytcore-ios-share&referringSource=articleShare

Fear of the near future, of what the Chinese state will do to capitalism rather than what capitalism will do to the Chinese state, is the sum of several fears. First, that the moral bankruptcy of the social credit system will weaken the creditworthiness of the financial system in China. Second, that lockdowns will shut down manufacturing in China. And third, that manufacturing jobs will leave China.

Fear of the near future tends to be as impractical as exuberance about the near future.

The two perpetuate certainty, leaving no room for doubt. They force inaction, paralyzing one with terror and tranquilizing the other with distraction. And they allow for an ignorance of history, causing us to miss the promise of our own times.

CHAPTER 3

Heroes and Villains and Miscellany

"All we can know is that we know nothing. And that's the height of human wisdom."

—Leo Tolstoy, *War and Peace*

The domes of Moscow's St. Basil's Cathedral are as incandescent as the Northern Lights. They are painted flame-like swirls of red, blue, bronze, gold, green, and white. They shine as an eternal flame, casting out the lights of all false religions and of all godless religions.

And yet the mystery of Russia, the riddle of her indomitable spirit, endures.

What also endures is a rot too widespread to reverse with words or weapons, though arms we need and bear. Despite differences of a continental and constitutional nature, events involving Russia [84]warrant our attention.

These events were the reason for my trip to Moscow. There, I participated in a series of private meetings with Putin opposition leaders and former Pennsylvania governor Tom Ridge.

In traveling with Governor Ridge, I had the honor to sit beside and listen to a man of immense poise and distinction. He honored me with his questions about Wall Street, listening to my answers as if I were one of his advisers, engaging me in conversation to and from our journey to Moscow.

The journey continued in Moscow, when the Russians came for us in ways we had not thought of—ways they knew we would not forget. Never will I forget Russia's wealth of tradition and poverty of trust. Nor will I forget the relics of a dead religion or the rituals on behalf of the enemy of religion. For while Lenin lies embalmed and entombed within Red Square, the dictatorship *over* the proletariat is far from dead.

Despite the fervency of the few, communism is not a threat to Russia's future. The present danger is instead the manifestation of one man's long memorandum from Moscow and his warnings about Moscow.

Because this man was not only right but just. Because he had a truth to issue, and he believed in the truth of a fundamental prop-

---

[84] Berman, Ilan L. "Russia's Propaganda Is More Persuasive Than We Think." American Foreign Policy Council, 5 January 2023, www.afpc.org/publications/articles/russias-propaganda-is-more-persuasive-than-we-think

osition: that sometimes party loyalty asks too much. Because he agreed with what John F. Kennedy had said about politics, Richard Nixon defied the politics of the moment and urged Americans (per the title of his final book[85]) to seize the moment. He urged them to not lose Russia.[86]

But lose it we did. Perhaps we were destined to lose what was never ours to win, because those who came to induce shock therapy left Russia in a state of shock.

Those who came bearing ideas—praising the idea about "the return to Europe"—had no idea about the people and politics of Russia.

Because the missionaries were economists with a certain idea not of Russia but of themselves. And their plans were like battle plans: unable to extend with certainty beyond the first encounter.

The economists were their own worst enemy.

Unaware of the reality of Russia—that ideologies expire but interests endure, that chief among these interests is Russian national interest—the economists, through a combination of arrogance and malpractice, failed to learn the lessons of *The Economic Consequences of the Peace*.[87]

In their attempt to replace *Homo Sovieticus* with *Homo economicus*, the economists of the West, with their reliance on for-

---

[85] Nixon, Richard. (1992). *Seize the Moment: America's Challenge in a One-Superpower World*. Richard Nixon Foundation. https://store.nixonfoundation.org/products/seize-the-moment

[86] Friedman, T. L. (1992, March 11). Nixon's "Save Russia" Memo: Bush Feels the Sting. The New York Times. Retrieved August 11, 2023, from https://www.nytimes.com/1992/03/11/world/nixon-s-save-russia-memo-bush-feels-the-sting.html

[87] Keynes, John Maynard. (1920). *The Economic Consequences of the Peace*. https://sourcebooks.fordham.edu/mod/1920keynes.asp

mulas and their formulaic approach to production at the cost of ignoring all other approaches to history and culture, in their zeal to reduce the complexity of man to the neatness of mathematics, the purveyors of shock therapy were the civilian predecessors of the U.S. military's use of shock and awe.

In the aftermath of a colossal military disaster, we would be wise to revisit what happened before we dropped 7,423 bombs in 365 days, in the second-to-last year of the longest war in U.S. history. This was a time before Operation Enduring Freedom became an ordeal and a test of endurance, lasting two decades and costing $2 trillion.

This was before we sought to liberate the same country Russia had failed to conquer. It was before the 43rd president pledged to end tyranny in our world, and before the 41st president pledged to embrace a "new world order"[88] freer from the threat of terror, stronger in the pursuit of justice, and more secure in the quest for peace.

Eleven years before 9/11, on September 11, 1990, President George H.W. Bush spoke about the world to come. His speech read like a response in the affirmative, a resolution not only *for* the Gulf War but a writ to end *all* wars, making the world safe for history. The speech turned a question mark into an exclamation point. And it answered a query ("The End of History?"[89]) with a rhapsody about prosperity and harmony.

Flash forward to June 16, 2001. President George W. Bush, whose father was a spokesman for supranational power, spoke

---

88 "Bush's Brave New World Order." *Air & Space Forces Magazine*, 1 August 2007, www.airandspaceforces.com/article/0807keeperfile/

89 Fukuyama, Francis. "The End of History?" *The National Interest*. No. 16, Summer 1989, pp. 3-18. www.wright.edu/~christopher.oldstone-moore/fukuyama.htm

(not for the last time) as if he had supernatural powers. About Vladimir Putin[90], Bush the Younger said:

I looked the man in the eye. I found him to be very straightforward and trustworthy. We had a very good dialogue. I was able to get a sense of his soul; a man deeply committed to his country and the best interests of his country.

Sixty-six days later, Bush looked the nation in the eye as he spoke about G-d. He condemned those who had blasphemed and betrayed G-d, assuring members of Congress, fellow citizens, and freedom-loving peoples throughout the world that G-d was on our side. He told the public that the outcome of the war on terror[91] was certain, because G-d is not neutral in the forever wars between freedom and fear, justice and cruelty.

Bush also praised Governor Ridge, who watched the speech from the House gallery alongside British Prime Minister Tony Blair, First Lady Laura Bush, New York Mayor Rudolph Giuliani, and New York Governor George Pataki. Bush called Ridge a military veteran, an effective governor, a true patriot, and a trusted friend.

"He will lead, oversee, and coordinate a comprehensive national strategy to safeguard our country against terrorism, and respond to any attacks that may come," Bush said.

Bush held these truths to be self-evident, certain of the virtues Ridge possesses. And what Bush said about Ridge—that he is a true patriot—I saw firsthand. While preparing to leave Russia, Ridge saved my friend and our colleague from the Russians. Headed toward our plane to leave Russia, the authorities

---

90 "Bush Saw Putin's Soul." *C-SPAN*, 17 June 2001, www.c-span.org/video/?c4718091/user-clip-bush-putins-soul

91 "Address to a Joint Session of Congress and the American People." *George W. Bush White House Archives*, 20 September 2001, https://georgewbush-whitehouse.archives.gov/news/releases/2001/09/print/20010920-8.html

yanked this colleague off the line for a last-minute harassment session.

Without Ridge, the Russians would have won. They would have detained my friend, a critic of Putin and an ally of justice, interrogating him first and charging him later. But because of Ridge, the plane stayed on the ground. We did not take off without our friend.

Despite the likely protestations of the pilot and orders from the control tower, my sky marshal—his badge, his body; his star, the Bronze Star—commandeered that plane with actions of bravery. The marshal, a man of moral health and martial vigor, seized my right forearm.

"Jason," he said, "we do not leave a man behind."

Where the governor went, I followed.

We returned to our seats on the plane with our friend.

Governor Ridge is a hero.

In his stead, the land—the homeland—has too many needs to meet and too few heroes to meet our needs. The land is unhappy, at home and abroad, as America talks and Russia acts. And now the chance for the leaders of both countries to meet jaw to jaw is over. America has no chance to jawbone Russia, and Russia has no need to chance the spoils of war with peace.

And so, the West watches as the man in the West Wing of the White House, the president of the United States, asks us to watch him speak about Russia's illegal annexation of Ukraine.

*

"Freedom to be your best means nothing unless you are willing to do your best."
—Colin Powell

Next to a historic courthouse stands a house of laws. The house is empty but not forgotten, closed but not condemned, uniting words of promise with a word for the Promised Land.

The house honors the spirit of the New World, of the will-to-do rather than the idleness-to-dream. The house makes real the promises of Washington, Adams, Jefferson, Madison, and Monroe. It evokes G-d's promise to Abraham and the promise of a martyr named Abraham, freeing a people from bondage and binding up the nation's wounds, thus establishing a house of Israel, Congregation Hope of Israel, in the new Israel of America.

So stands the house in which a boy brought the lights, where a couple's only son kept the lights in accordance with the law. So stands the house in which a future soldier toiled, from which a four-star general heard the trumpet call.

Now the trumpet summons us to stand and mourn the passing of Colin L. Powell. Let us also mourn the passing of Secretary Powell's neighborhood[92], recognizing that the hope still lives and the work—the work to repair this section of the world—must not die.

It survives in works that depict great moments in the life of America, from the arrival of the founder of the Bronx to the departure of the Father of Our Country, from a battle for the life of our country to a scene honoring our greatest Founding Father.

---

92 Hampson, Rick. "The General From South Bronx—Little Evidence Of Colin Powell Remains In Old Neighborhood." *Seattle Times*, 10 February 1991, https://archive.seattletimes.com/archive/?date=19910210&slug=1265511

The work survives as murals inside the first floor of the Bronx County Courthouse. There, tour guides hold court and court an audience, so all Americans may see Powell's story in themselves. This way, his story of service, of courage in war and justice in peace, may flourish.

Across from the courthouse, in Joyce Kilmer Park, a symbol of beauty survives. The Statue of Lorelei stands as a maiden in marble, a fountain with decorations of mermaids, sirens, and seashells. Nothing else stands in this section of Powell's neighborhood, because the legacy of the Grand Concourse is, alas, far from grand.

The opportunity for renewal is in the fact that this neighborhood is one of seventy-five Opportunity Zones[93] in the Bronx alone. And investing in Opportunity Zones is a chance to create a living monument, allowing people in a neighborhood to form a community.

This chance—to revive a community—is the chance to return Secretary Powell to his community. Doing so blesses his memory by building on his legacy, complementing his acts for Hope of Israel with acts of our own, and continues his support for the State of Israel with our investments in these United States.

Secretary Powell is a hero.

*

"We shape our buildings; thereafter they shape us."

—Winston Churchill

[93] "Opportunity Zone Program." *Empire State Development*, https://esd.ny.gov/sites/default/files/FINAL-Recommendations-OZ-42618.pdf

Beneath a ceiling of green and gold and a canopy of stars lies a grand concourse—the Main Concourse—of Grand Central Terminal. Here, all traffic is foot traffic from which commuters pass, and below which passenger trains come and go.

Beneath this backdrop of marble and brass, below which lines shine like silver and speed like quicksilver, trains arrive and depart according to the times on the schedule board. This is a temple to Mercury, where a statue of Mercury stands outside, above time, with Hercules and Minerva at his feet.

So stands the Glory of Commerce, safe from those men who are neither good nor wise. So stands the backdrop for my story about a man who heads north as his character heads south.

And so begins his departure on the New Haven Line, ending with his obsession over bloodlines, for his descent is rapid and sad.

His descent saddens me because I can no longer think of Wall Street in a certain way, in which the lines in a story about money and service and class—lines as long as this man's lineage and as straight as words on ruled paper—make sense. These lines do not suit him. They hang like chains from his sack suit, resounding with the verdict of history:

Thou art weighed in the balance and found wanting.

For want of faith in the conviction of truth, and because of his conviction that all peoples of a particular faith have an aversion to truth, that a minority in all nations save one are loyal to the one nation in which they are not a minority, this man believes that no person of the Jewish faith, neither by right of birth nor by rites of naturalization, can be a true American. He believes that I am therefore un-American, because I am in and among the money changers, but not of the houses of old money. To him, "the Jews" do not belong, and I have no right to go. And while Jews put Israel first, Israel has no right to be.

Not for the last time would I hear such things.

But this was the first time someone—a coworker—had uttered such a thing to my face. His words were an attempt to save face, all because of what our mutual employer had said about me. Because my name was on the intraoffice roll call of names, and because I was one of the past month's top performers, my success was proof of—in this man's eyes—my failings as a person.

He saw me as the other.

If he saw the worst in me, I saw nothing good in him. And if together we saw past each other, then we were both blind.

We were not, however, both lost. For he found what he wanted and saw what he believed: confirmation of the goodness of his bias against Jews.

If he saw me as a creature of stratagems and spoils, with a spirit as dull as night, I saw him as a traitor to his class. I saw him squander his gifts and forsake his requirements, with hypocrisy toward the honorable and heresy in the house of a life-giving G-d.

Here, after all, was a man who had tread upon the flags of G-d and country, trampled on the land where his fathers died—the land of the Pilgrims' pride—despite his Pilgrim ancestry.

Here was a villain who had visited his sins upon his forefathers.

*

> **"There is a land of the living and a land of the dead and the bridge is love, the only survival, the only meaning."**
> —Thornton Wilder

The towers stand as bowed string instruments of concrete and metal. Cables run from the base to the pegs, while sliders pass through archways made by the inclination of bow and strings.

They stand as harps in symphony of man and nature, with cables running parallel from the top to the deck. They are giant fiddles—the haegeum of the East—summoning the bonghwang, a mythical bird of eternal life.

The towers bridge the distance between the island and the mainland. The Incheon Bridge[94] appears and the lights of Seoul glow red, yellow, blue, pink, green, and white.

---

[94] Incheon Bridge Photo: Incheon bridge 2009 [Photograph]. Retrieved from Wikimedia Commons: https://en.wikipedia.org/wiki/Incheon#/media/File%3AIncheon_bridge_2009.jpg

Passengers see the lights—many, myself included, for the first time—from the windows of a wide-body airliner in which the fin and rudder bear the symbol of motion and signify the spirit of pioneers. There in the sky I remove the printout[95] from my shirt pocket and compare darkness on paper with a profusion of exterior lights. And I see the contrast of one body and two states—of North Korea at night and South Korea during any hour of the day. It is a snapshot of the battle between lies and truth.

95 Yulsman, Tom. "The Two Koreas: Like Night and Day." *Discover*, 31 May 2013, www.discovermagazine.com/environment/the-two-koreas-like-night-and-day

The lights put the lie to the division between the Global North and the Global South, because the line between the two, the Brandt Line[96], is false.

The line looks seismic but labels the poor static, consigning all Korea and 130 other countries to economic backwardness.

The lights belie the idea that history stops, that nothing exists except an endless present, because present-day Seoul looks like a futuristic city. And the lights of the Digital Media City (DMC[97]) exemplify this look. Masts mimic paper and the roof of Seoul World Cup Stadium looks like a paper kite—a shield kite—above a field of green and white.

The lights are everywhere, from the top of the Olympic Bridge[98] to the roof of Seoul's tallest building. They shine like a torch and glow like a lantern, lighting a path to the future.

---

96 Brandt Report Image: The Brandt Line [Image]. Retrieved from Wikimedia Commons: https://en.wikipedia.org/wiki/Brandt_Report#/media/File%3AThe_Brandt_Line.png

97 "Digital Media City." *Visit Seoul*, 14 November 2017, https://english.visitseoul.net/attractions/Digital-Media-City_/11145

98 Olympic Bridge Image: [Image]. Retrieved from Google Images: https://images.app.goo.gl/nYZYp2JwKtdsSkBj9

But sometimes the past invades the present, requiring all good men to arm themselves with the mace of honor and the lights of truth.

The lights also shine inside the plenary chamber of the National Assembly Building, where the ceiling lights match the days in a year. Each light is a star, and the stars number four constellations plus a long dozen—or 365 points of light for 300 legislators with multiple points of view.

The building, with its white exterior and blue dome, looks like a planetarium. But the interior has no star chamber, because people are free to observe democracy in action. It is a house of construction, just as Seoul is a city alive with construction. In Seoul, citizens work to bridge their differences and sustain the city's network of bridges.

The bridges remind me of another bridge—a footbridge in Manhattan—between Park Avenue and Grand Central Terminal. This bridge, the Pershing Square Viaduct,[99] bears the name of John J. Pershing, General of the Armies and commander of the American Expeditionary Forces (AEF) during the Great War. It spans no river, though it has strategic value just the same. What civilians would demolish with words, no commander would speak of destroying except in war.

---

[99] Holth, Nathan. "Park Avenue Viaduct." *Historic Bridges*, 2 September 2019, https://historicbridges.org/bridges/browser/?bridgebrowser=newyork/parkavenueviaductgrandcentral/

In other words: do not burn a bridge of friendship or opportunity. Instead, look at the faces of the people on the bridge, the people going by. Perhaps an old acquaintance—a face of days of auld lang syne—will appear. The face may be a harbinger of success or a herald of salvation, recalling the concept of face. This concept is central to the life and soul of South Korea, as my story of an after-work dinner, or hoesik, demonstrates.

Ceremony defines this dinner. It begins with the pouring of the first drink—with not only *who* holds the bottle but how one holds it (with two hands)—and the lifting of glasses and wording of a toast.

Each course is an act of ceremony. There is ceremony in the cooking and savoring of each course, and the mood is convivial while the air smells combustible. There is the potency of soju, with the empty bottles standing like bowling pins—some upright and others leaning against one another. And there is the intense aroma of the soju—the smell of gasoline—the smell of smoke, the amplitude of sound, and the air with qualities like a racing engine.

As the dinner proceeds, so does the drinking. And while I am happy to raise a glass and toast with a sip of water or juice, I am not much of a drinker. I did, however, observe the rites of a host, so as not to offend the host of a dinner in my honor. I measured my intake, not because I have a proclivity for excess or a fondness for excessive drinking, but because I have little tolerance or taste for alcohol.

I aim to never be inhospitable, so I would not insult another man's hospitality. Thus I would indulge my appetite rather than slake my thirst.

Were it the other way around, I doubt I would have had the sobriety to know the difference between munificence and malice. I doubt I would have cared to see the difference between the goodness of my host and the wickedness of those who gave to him what he presented to me, repackaging the oldest hatred in new threads of linen, leather, and gold.

Beneath the glitter lay a hardcover book. It was a Korean translation of a Russian work of propaganda and lies: *The Protocols of the Elders of Zion*.

Except for *Mein Kampf*, Hitler's autobiography of delusion and prophecy of annihilation, the *Protocols* is the most infamous and libelous expression of anti-Semitism known to man.

Faced with either looking at the book or looking away from it and causing my host to lose face, I rose and delivered a rousing speech on behalf of the men in the room and the citizens of South Korea.

Two days later, the same executive asked me to meet him in his office.

He bowed when he saw me, surprising me with his mien of sorrow and shame. I did not know—not at the outset, at least—that this meeting was, to him, as grave as any loss and as solemn as any graveside sermon. For he had not known the history of the

Protocols, or the history wrought due to the *Protocols*[100]. And he did not know the history of anti-Semitism.

He had never been to a synagogue, as there were none in South Korea. (Though now there is one,[101] a Chabad house, in Seoul.) And in a country with less than 1,000 Jews, he had never met a Jew. (Though philo-Semitism (admiration and respect for Jews) is strong throughout South Korea.)

He offered an explanation, not an excuse, for his behavior.

I told him his behavior was excusable and his explanation understandable. I too had ignored the idiom to judge not, to not judge a book by its cover.

That this book's cover was decorative was proof of the book's power to deceive. Not only that, but its pages contained the featural script of the Korean alphabet and retained few of the images, neither medieval nor modern, of Jews as hideous and subhuman. The book looked both rare and respectable, so much so that the man standing before me had not given it a second look. He believed its tale of a conspiracy to take over the world and he wanted to be a part of it. He wanted me to give him access and share the secret handshakes that did not exist.

My explanation did not assuage the man's sadness. He believed the book to be true and felt I either did not have the connections he thought I had or would not open those doors to him. He was frustrated with the history lesson I shared with him regarding what the book was truly about.

---

100 Starr, Michael. "'Elders Of Zion' book being sold by top booksellers." *The Jerusalem Post*, 26 January 2022, https://stgdesktopcore.jpost.com/diaspora/antisemitism/article-694559

101 Dolstein, Josefin. "What it's like to be Jewish in South Korea." *Times of Israel*, 3 February 2018, www.timesofisrael.com/what-its-like-to-be-jewish-in-south-korea/

Not until I talked to him about the bridges of Seoul did he begin to relax. Not until I told him about the other bridge, the Pershing Square Viaduct, did he know I was his friend.

He listened to my story of a chance encounter on the bridge, where I saw the person who had run the training program at Cantor Fitzgerald. The *very same* person who shredded the letter inviting me to interview for the program, who told me to leave and not return—because he did not hire anyone with a liberal arts degree.

To say he had a reputation among trainees, that he was as brusque to them as he was to his own colleagues, would be kind. And his brilliance was undeniable, just as his arrogance, worsened by the fact that he knew we knew he was brilliant, was (for many) unbearable.

When he was not telling us that he had graduated from an Ivy League school, or schooling us by shouting at us, he was telling us to stop wasting his time. But when he shouted at me during our interview, I shouted back. That made all the difference.

“Kid, don’t get smart with me,” he said.

“My name is Jason,” I said.

“I don’t care. Tell me, what’s 347 times eleven.”

“Three thousand eight hundred seventeen.”

“Divided by three.”

“One thousand two hundred seventy-two and three tenths.”

“Give me the square root.”

"Give me a calculator, the one you're holding."

"I like you, Jason," he said.

High praise indeed. Because no one else talked to or back at him. When we met on the bridge, he congratulated me on my success and marveled at our mutual luck to have not been there that day in September. He later referred clients to me and became a good friend.

My new friend, the man in Seoul, valued the story.

"It was an honor to listen to you. You honor me."

"Friend, we honor each other," I said.

"Thank you, Jason."

*

"He who passively accepts evil is as much involved in it as he who helps to perpetrate it. He who accepts evil without protesting against it is really cooperating with it."

—Martin Luther King Jr.

Complicity colors life gray with resignation until artificial light is the only light people know. Complicity conditions people to know not what they see until all life is a series of compromises. Complicity worsens over time until people know nothing at all.

As complicity spreads within the world of finance and investing, minor returns—mediocre results—assume major proportions.

Think of the accountant who talks in numbers, not percentages. He who makes thousands seem like millions while a few thousand dollars mean nothing to most millionaires. This makes the accountant's acumen (at best) average, as a client with a net worth of $20 million profits little from paying $3,000 less in taxes.

The money matters, and the savings count. But neither matters enough for us to revere the accountant.

But because of the age we live in, where minimal effort creates maximum pressure, the fastest way to relieve the pressure we feel is to do what the accountant says. And unless we go from resignation to resolve and press for answers to the questions we must ask, we will never get what we deserve. We must refuse to go away, applying pressure rather than acquiescing to it. If we don't, we will never know what we deserve.

For we deserve all the money we can save. This way, we may increase our security while providing for the beneficiaries of our largesse. And we can name the beneficiaries—specifying who will get what—in a life insurance contract.

We deserve the chance to leave a legacy, so our deeds may give life to our dreams.

But to do so requires a full accounting of the choices available to us. Only then can we make an informed decision about where to invest.

Without the ability to judge our choices and limit our exposure to chance, we have no choice but to look elsewhere. And we *must* look elsewhere, because it is not enough for an accountant to advise us, or a lawyer to counsel us, or a financial adviser to consult us. The information we have is not all the information we need.

And yet we must also recognize how little we know. Most of us, for example, do not understand the income tax system or know how much tax we owe (especially owners of digital assets, most of whom are unintentional tax cheats). Most of us pay someone whose job it is to study and decipher the code, whose job causes us to mistake the ordinary for the extraordinary. It's as if their calculator were godly, the paper roll sacred, and the green eyeshade holy. As if the accountant were an apostle of faith and service.

None of us should pay an accountant who cannot explain his services. The same is true for a lawyer who cannot explain his bill without billing for additional services, or an adviser who cannot explain anything without trying to sell something in the process.

All of us have a right to a thorough explanation.

*

"No man should receive a dollar unless that dollar has been fairly earned."

—Theodore Roosevelt

Just as money comes in different denominations, different designations govern the money supply.

But what an individual can see, or what an institution can measure, is different from what other individuals and institutions can do with an investor's money. And no, what is legible on paper or countable as paper money does not count when Wall Street devalues the currency of language.

The phenomenon of soft dollars—in which institutional investors use a percentage of brokerage fees to buy research rather than returning or reinvesting the money—is legal. But it's also wrong.

When every extra cent a brokerage firm charges has nothing to do with the cost of executing a trade, problems arise. The same is true when all those extra cents amount to tens of thousands of dollars. Or when, for the sake of argument, the cost of a million-dollar trade is $40,000 and half the cost goes to something else—something an institutional investor wants but his clients do not need.

The chief problem is that an institutional investor has no moral right to pay for his wants with another man's wallet. It is immoral to buy research from a brokerage firm or use research as a catch-all for personal spending. And yet, it's done because the law does not forbid it.

Put another way, the right to act is not an a priori argument that an action is right. By what right, after all, is an institutional investor right to be generous with other people's money? And by what right is he right to be prudent with his own money and profligate with money he does not own?

How can he who argues the law and dismisses the facts[102]—when the facts reveal the use of soft dollars to fly traders from Boston to Bermuda on a private jet—purchase tickets to sporting events, or buy gifts?

Nothing is right, straight, or square about this situation.

Nothing is fair or new about a deal that relaxes the rigid integrity necessary for honesty in business and service of the public good.

Nothing is sound, as Theodore Roosevelt[103] would say, about a theory that fails the test of actual experience, because an ounce of performance is worth a ton of promise.

We need not wonder what Roosevelt would say about corruption that weakens the fiber of a community and wounds the character

---

[102] Moyer, Lisa. "The End Of Easy Money." *Forbes*, 12 January 2007, www.forbes.com/2007/01/11/sec-soft-money-hedge-biz-cx_lm_0112sec.html

[103] *Mr. Roosevelt in Montevideo*. November 5, 1913. Sagamore Hill National Historic Site. https://www.theodorerooseveltcenter.org/Research/Digital-Library/Record?libID=o279226. Theodore Roosevelt Digital Library. Dickinson State University.

of men. Even in his sleep, between the place of his death and his final resting place, he speaks to us still. He would, I believe, oppose soft dollars with vigor equal to his vehemence of the father of dollar diplomacy[104], saying:

We shall never make our republic what it should be until as a people we thoroughly understand and put in practice the doctrine that success is abhorrent if attained by the sacrifice of the fundamental principles of morality.

We have a duty to abide by Roosevelt's words[105].

*

"A pen is certainly an excellent instrument to fix a man's attention and to inflame his ambition."

—John Adams

East of Los Angeles Street and the Fashion District of Los Angeles, east of the city in which the ragman plies his trade and the present sounds like the past, east of the factories and warehouses, lies West Babylon, Long Island, and seven cities of the dead.

The cities include New Montefiore Cemetery, where my paternal grandfather, Philip Mandel, speaks to me in his sleep. For a dozen years he lay silent, from the second week of the first month of the year, January 11, 1987, till the final decade of the twentieth century. It was then I flew to Los Angeles to sign an important contract and begin life as an entrepreneur.

---

[104] *Milestones in the History of U.S. Foreign Relations: Dollar Diplomacy, 1909-1913*. Office of the Historian, Foreign Service Institute. https://history.state.gov/milestones/1899-1913/dollar-diplo. United States Department of State.

[105] Coenn, Daniel. (2014). *Theodore Roosevelt: His Words*. BookRix. https://books.google.com/books/about/Theodore_Roosevelt.html?id=IpYJBAAAQBAJ

My family mourned for seven days, plus twoscore days and nights, until the morning of the forty-eighth day, February 28, 1987. Then, in accordance with my grandfather's wishes, I honored his memory and acted my age—the age of religious majority—and had my bar mitzvah.

Seven years after I was the age of majority—twenty-five—my grandfather spoke to me in writing. He told me to "get it in writing." In this case "it" meant words on paper, a legally binding contract, rather than words alone.

If I had something in writing in the first place, I would not have been in Los Angeles trying to close a deal and raise money. I would not be verifying what my then-business partner said was true, or what I trusted was true because of what he said to me. I would not need to confirm that he had $30 million from institutional investors for us to manage.

Had I not gotten this deal in writing, I would not have gotten what I needed most: a pen.

I needed a pen because I could not find my own, the one with a star on top I thought I needed to impress clients, the star symbolizing a snowcap and the cap representing the peak of Mont Blanc by Montblanc. I needed *any pen*—to sign the contract before me.

What I needed lay inside the drawer of a credenza I had never seen before, beneath a tangle of wires and a thicket of parts. It was a click pen of a clicker, a talisman with the power to conjure the past. It produced light like a magic lantern. The light shone on slides of machines, molds, presses, feathers, and hats. It passed through photographs of my grandfather's life. It revealed scenes from the life of my grandfather's career at the Mangrove Feather Company.

My grandfather started the company when he was twenty-five.

I started my company, and made my first million dollars, at the same age.

I founded my company by finding my grandfather, by feeling his presence and sharing his company while finalizing my first big deal.

I used his pen—a pen no one else had ever seen or touched—to write my future. I used a pen he sent out as a gift to customers in 1981 (eighteen years prior to that meeting) that was hidden in that credenza, and no one at my client's company could explain how it got there or had ever seen the pen before. I knew it was a message from him—from my grandfather. I knew he was with me then, and he has guarded over me all the days of my life even after his passing on January 11, 1987.

CHAPTER 4

Miracle

"Israel was not created in order to disappear—Israel will endure and flourish. It is the child of hope and the home of the brave. It can neither be broken by adversity nor demoralized by success. It carries the shield of democracy and it honors the sword of freedom."

—John F. Kennedy

Between the kingdoms of life and a kingdom of eternal life, between the universe and the King of the universe, between cosmology and theology, commonality exists.

Between them, each member of each group is a person of faith. And no person is without faith, not even an atheist. For there is far too much that is impossible without faith.

No person alive today, whether he is a scientist in Israel or an Israeli citizen with a passion for science and religion, would be in Israel if not for the faith of the founding fathers of the State of Israel.

In Israel, faith exists—faiths coexist—as a synthesis of symbols and sounds. This faith encompasses the Muslim crescent to the Christian cross to the Jewish star, from calls to prayer to prayers for hope, with “The Hope” (“Haktivah”) playing within the hearts and souls of a free people in their own land.

Coexistence might at times seems impossible—and so too might existence in the face of Israel’s war dead. But when the families of the fallen say coexistence is impossible, that Arabs cannot be Israelis and Israelis cannot include Christians and Muslims and Arabic-speaking Druze, look again at the multiplicity of faiths throughout Israel. For you will see that coexistence is indeed possible.

The lights of monotheism shine unto the nation of Israel. They still shine, such that tomorrow is today and next year is now, making this year—and all the years since the first year of Israel’s independence—a festival of lights. These lights prove the desire is no dream, because Israel is real and Jerusalem is the capital of Israel.

About the reality of Israel, no matter how much it aligns with a writer’s vision of a homeland in *The Jewish State*[106] or differs from an artist’s vision of “the new Jew”[107] in a Jewish homeland, the truth is in the numbers.

The truth is that the security of Israel is the story (in part) of investment securities and the success of Israel Bonds. Founded in 1950, two years after the birth of a new nation, conceived in liberty, and dedicated to the natural right of the Jewish people to be masters of their own fate, the bonds of affection within Israel are as strong as America’s affection for Israel and Israel Bonds.

---

[106] Herzl, Theodor. (1896). *The Jewish State*. www.gutenberg.org/ebooks/25282

[107] Sayers, John. “Zionism and Art: Bezalel Narkiss Speaks in ‘Israel at 50’ Series.” *Library of Congress*, August 1998, www.loc.gov/loc/lcib/9808/narkiss.html

Thanks to America, the well-wisher to the freedom and independence of all, Israel is free and independent. And thanks to one night in America, Israel knows why the night of May 10, 1951, is different from all other nights.

On that night, three and a half hours from its second year as a member of the United Nations, and three and a half days from its third year as a nation, at 8:30 p.m. Eastern Daylight Time, the premier venue in New York City hosted the premiere of a global performance.

On that night, seven years and two days after the unconditional surrender of Nazi Germany and the end of World War II in Europe, after the defeat of the enemy and reports detailing the criminality of conditions borne by survivors of the enemy's separate war against the Jewish people, after bearing witness to the conditions himself, going where "Old Blood and Guts" could not go without vomiting, after General Dwight D. Eisenhower toured the Ohrdruf[108] concentration camp at Buchenwald and

[108] "What We Fought Against: Ohrdruf." *The National WWII Museum*, 4 April 2020, www.nationalww2museum.org/war/articles/ohrdruf-concentration-camp

saw the remains of the dead and the sunken faces of the living dead, after nights of terror and years of tyranny, from the Night of Long Knives to the Night of Broken Glass, the night felt like the dawn of Liberation Day.

On that night, 20,000 people raised $35 million[100] for Israel Bonds.

The night was a testament of faith. Not in terms of religion—though many of the attendees were of the same religion—but in terms of investing. How else to describe the purchase of securities from a country whose security at the time was uncertain? How else to describe faith in redemption at the time of maturity, when Israel was young and poor?

How else to describe faith in paper promises and drawings on paper certificates, of vignettes drawn from the Bible and of visions of a people drawn to the Promised Land, when at the time Israel was a dreamland?

In the end, how else to describe faith in an image of Israel, when at the time Israel was a stranger in a strange and hostile land?

These questions, of course, are rhetorical. Certain investments defy reason and redound to the credit of the person who provides credit. And certain investments bear the full faith and credit of a person's belief in the survival and success of liberty.

*

109 "Ben Gurion Opens Israel Bond Campaign in New York; $35,000,000 Raised at Rally." *Jewish Telegraphic Agency*, 11 May 1951, www.jta.org/archive/ben-gurion-opens-israel-bond-campaign-in-new-york-35000000-raised-at-rally

"Again, you can't connect the dots looking forward; you can only connect them looking backward. So you have to trust that the dots will somehow connect in your future. You have to trust in something—your gut, destiny, life, karma, whatever."

—Steve Jobs

The line between a night in honor of Israel and life in present-day Israel is now clear.

The line, like the lights on the night of May 10, 1951, radiates from an arena with an arched marquee.

Beneath the downlights of the marquee, beneath the aura of triumph and the halo of glory, every man enters a hall of mirrors—a corridor of glass windows—before entering Madison Square Garden.

The image of this entrance outlives the life of this arena.[110] But no one can forget the images and stories of this arena.

In this arena, where the living had gathered to mourn the dead and warn the world, bidding Americans beware the ides of March, the American Jewish Congress and the Jewish Labor Committee held a "Boycott Nazi Germany"[111] rally on March 15, 1937.

In this arena, where 40,000 people gathered to mourn 2 million Jewish dead, bidding Americans beware the enormity of a crime

---

[110] "History of Madison Square Garden." *Madison Square Garden Entertainment*, www.msg.com/madison-square-garden/history

[111] "Anti-Nazis hold demonstration." *From Haven to Home: A Library of Congress Exhibition Marking 350 Years of Jewish Life in America" at the Library of Congress*, 2004, www.loc.gov/item/96520472/

without a name, organizers held a *We Will Never Die*[112] protest on March 9, 1943.

In this arena—where Jews gathered to protest for right, with firmness *in the right*—the friends of the Reich also gathered on February 20, 1939[113].

Looking back on those years, who believed that some of the Jewish people would not die? Who believed that some survivors would live in freedom, or that the world would have a new birth of freedom? Who believed that the days of the years of Israel would surpass threescore years and ten, and that Israel would survive and succeed?

The questions seem to beggar belief.

Next came the aftermath of war in Europe and the outbreak of war in the Middle East. There, the enemies of the Nazis barred survivors of the Nazis entry to Mandatory Palestine, and London ordered Jerusalem to attack the descendants of the ruler of Jerusalem. British warships fired on a refugee ship, and the question became whether the passengers aboard the *Exodus*, heirs to the Israelites in the Book of Exodus, would find refuge in their biblical homeland.

The most important question was whether Jewish soldiers would repel the invasion of Israel by the forces of Egypt, Syria, Iraq, Lebanon, Saudi Arabia, Yemen, and Transjordan.

How Israel would prevail was a separate question. The fourth and final question was whether the world would see the raising of

---

112 "The 'We Will Never Die' Pageant." *United States Holocaust Memorial Museum, Washington, DC*, 17 September 2021, https://encyclopedia.ushmm.org/content/en/article/the-we-will-never-die-pageant

113 Kramer, Sarah Kate. "When Nazis Took Manhattan." *NPR*, 20 February 2019, www.npr.org/sections/codeswitch/2019/02/20/695941323/when-nazis-took-manhattan

the Israeli flag—the Ink Flag[114]—in the Negev, signaling not only victory in war but also vindication in peace.

The question was whether the words of a prophet and the promise of a prime minister would be one, with soldiers beating swords into plowshares and making the desert bloom.

The question of how the Jewish state would be at peace with itself, what with the expulsion and evacuation of the Jews of the Arab states, was also unanswerable at the time of Israel's independence.

The question was not when the answers would come, but rather: What will the answers be? Would faith suffice or would the Jews of Israel make G-d's work their own? Would the Word begin the day or deeds keep it? Would the nations of the world

---

[114] Glatt, Benjamin. "Today in History: Winning Eilat with an ink flag." *The Jerusalem Post*, 10 March 2016, www.jpost.com/christian-news/today-in-history-winning-eilat-with-an-ink-flag-447516

eulogize Israel? Or would Jews throughout the world never let Israel die?

Looking back, the dots of life, love, and fate connect as constellations. The future appears as an expression of His will, for He counts the number of stars. He calls them all by their names, and He gives the people of Israel an everlasting name.

*

"In Israel, in order to be a realist, you must believe in miracles."

—David Ben-Gurion

By looking back through the historian's inverted telescope, we may see how irrelevant Arthur Koestler's observations of Israel look. Were Koestler to look through the telescope a second time, the view would not resemble his portrait[115] of Tel Aviv, of streets with no skyline and a coastline with nothing but sordid little cafes.

Were he to look at the circle, square, and triangle towers of Azrieli Center, the spiral tower unfurling like a scroll[116] of glass, he would see the rise of the tallest building in Israel. And at the very top of that building, he would have a 360-degree view of Tel Aviv, stretching from the holy city of Jerusalem to the Mediterranean Sea.

---

115 Holmes, Oliver. "'Stubbornly fighting for life': how Arthur Koestler reported the birth of Israel." *The Guardian*, 9 May 2018, www.theguardian.com/world/2018/may/09/stubbornly-fighting-for-life-how-arthur-koestler-reported-the-birth-of-israel

116 Walsh, Niall Patrick. "KPF's Spiraling Scroll Tower will be the Tallest Building in Tel Aviv." *ArchDaily*, 20 December 2018, www.archdaily.com/908223/kpfs-spiraling-scroll-tower-will-be-the-tallest-building-in-tel-aviv

Were Koestler to look for a Hebrew translation of his novel, *Darkness at Noon*[117], he would find readers of the Russian translation too. In fact, he would find 900,000 Russian-speaking Jews in Israel, or over a million Russian-speaking Israelis, all former captives of a dead empire and an evil ideology.

He would find the Soviet dissidents—the refuseniks—who would not die. He would find scientists, authors, leaders, giants, and statesmen. He would even find them all in one man, Natan Sharansky,[118] who stands *like* Stephen Douglas, the Little Giant, but stands *for* the principles of Abraham Lincoln, the tallest giant in the history of America.

Were Koestler to look by listening, translating sound into sight, he would hear the bang from the belly of an incoming airplane.

And were he among the passengers aboard an El Al[119] 747-200, he would hear the pangs of childbirth and the arrival of two new

---

117 Wilentz, Sean. "Darkness at Noon, Arthur Koestler (1940)." *Tablet*, 17 September 2013, www.tabletmag.com/sections/news/articles/darkness-at-noon-arthur-koestler-1940

118 "Natan Sharansky." *The Institute for the Study of Global Antisemitism and Policy (ISGAP)*, https://isgap.org/about/staff/natan-sharansky/

119 "Goodbye 747: El Al Bids Farewell to the Jumbo." *El Al*, www.elal.com/en/About-ELAL/About-ELAL/News/Pages/747-Farewell.aspx

passengers. He would find 1,086 passengers at the outset and 1,088 at the end of a single flight, or thirty-five flights in thirty-six hours, bringing 14,325 fellow travelers to freedom.

He would find Ethiopian Jews arriving at Ben Gurion Airport, courtesy of Operation Solomon.[120] He would find a freedom trail of gossamer thread, taking families out of Africa—from the Horn of Africa—to a land of plenty. On top of that, he would find military cargo planes returning from Africa, bearing precious cargo, according to the Law of Return.[121]

But let us not leave Tel Aviv or leave Koestler be just yet. First, let him also admire Tel Aviv University.

Let him look upon the towers of a temple[122] and the brilliance of a cloud[123], the latter gold in daylight and white during twilight. Let him walk inside and wander among the stars, free of any checkpoints, so he may explore the Check Point Institute for Information Security. There he will see a building reflective of Israeli society. A building whose exterior is abstract but adaptable, while the people inside—leaders in software engineering and computer science—change society with breakthroughs in robotics, visual computing, cloud computing, computational biology, and machine learning.

Let him also enter a house of worship, the Cymbalista Synagogue and Jewish Heritage Center, where the light comes from above. Let him see the light and the truth, so he may find his way back to Jewish life.

---

[120] "Operation Solomon, Ben Gurion Airport, Israel 1991." *The Jewish Lens*, www.jewishlens.org/photos/operation-solomon-ben-gurion-airport-israel-1991/

[121] "The Law of Return." *The Jewish Agency for Israel*, https://archive.jewishagency.org/first-steps/program/5131

[122] "The Cymbalista Synagogue and Jewish Heritage Center." *Tel Aviv University*, https://english.tau.ac.il/campus/cymbalista_center

[123] "Check Point Building." *Architect*, www.architectmagazine.com/project-gallery/check-point-building_o

Finally, let him read the Hebrew inscription—שויתי יהוה לנגדי תמיד—above the Torah ark, so he may say, "I have set the LORD always before me."

May the light[124] surrounding the ark guide him home.

*

"In Israel, a land lacking in natural resources, we learned to appreciate our greatest national advantage: our minds. Through creativity and innovation, we transformed barren deserts into flourishing fields and pioneered new frontiers in science and technology."

—Shimon Peres

In the beginning was the work. The work was hard, and the work was a national hardship.

The work would either save and transform Israel's economy or cost Prime Minister Peres his job and leave more people jobless.

The work had to free Israel's economy from "taxation without legislation,"[125] thus ending inflation before inflation ended Israel. The goal was to end the misery of 1984–reversing the indices by which economists measure misery—before record-high unemployment and runaway inflation left Israel with the economic structure of *1984*. This was to be accomplished before excessive spending left Israel with nothing but insurmountable debt.

---

124 "The Synagogue and Auditorium." *The Cymbalista Synagogue and Jewish Heritage Center | Tel Aviv University*, https://en-heritage.m.tau.ac.il/Synagogue

125 Mecha's Random Videos. (2018, October 30). *Inflation Is Taxation Without Representation—Milton Friedman* [Video]. YouTube. https://youtu.be/QDx68vE8qDI

The work began with the help of Herbert Stein[126], chairman of the Council of Economic Advisers under the one president who had risked everything to save Israel's life. A president who, while fighting to save the life of his administration, and later fighting—silently yet steadfastly—to save his own life while touring the Middle East, supplied Israel with the tools to finish the job.

Because of Richard Nixon's[127] help during the Yom Kippur War, Stein was able to help Israel wage war on inflation. As an Israelite among the Jews of Israel and an American in the Land of Israel, Stein was among friends.

Because he was an ally, he had the authority to recommend—and the discipline to demand—change.

A realist like Nixon, Stein had a vision of Israel. And as an idealist like the leader of the Israelites, Stein had a series of commandments for Israel.

His plan, also known as "Herb's 10 Points,"[128] was a decalogue of tight money, financial independence, and fiscal restraint. Economists in Israel and economic advisers to Israel's then-prime minister had made many of the same points. But where they failed, either for want of power or the will to speak truth to power, Stein succeeded.

He represented not only the arsenal of democracy, but the chief armorer of the only democracy in the Middle East. He represented the most powerful nation in the world.

---

[126] Fischer, Stanley. "Remembering Herb Stein: His Contributions as an Economist." *International Monetary Fund*, 6 January 2001, www.imf.org/en/News/Articles/2015/09/28/04/53/sp010601

[127] "The Yom Kippur War: 40 Years of Survival." *Richard Nixon Foundation*, 11 October 2016, www.nixonfoundation.org/2016/10/yom-kippur-war-40-years-survival/

[128] Fischer, 2001

Behind him lay the executive branch of the federal government: the State Department, the Pentagon, the Treasury, the White House, the Cabinet of the United States. Before him lay the instruments of diplomacy, law, commerce, and trade.

By adopting Stein's points, Israel conquered inflation. They went from 445 percent inflation[129] in 1984 to zero inflation in July 1986.

In Israel as it was in Europe, America was the author of reform. In 1984 as it was in 1948, America was the advocate of recovery. And in the time of Herbert Stein as it was in the time of Truman, Eisenhower, Marshall, and MacArthur, America was the apostle of repair.

In the busiest places—from the Old City to the first Hebrew city to the old port cities—the economy is strong. The cities rise with the sand sea, turning silica into silicon and the Israeli coastal plain into Silicon Wadi.[130] Thus marks the rise of the start-up nation,[131] where technology thrives.

Thus marks the corollary to Silicon Valley, similar in climate—both Mediterranean—while the one *bordering* the Mediterranean similarly features the likes of Apple, Microsoft, Google, Intel, Facebook, and IBM.

Strong in cybersecurity and AI, Israel's ace is in the ACES (autonomous, connected, electrified, and shared) revolution in the auto-

---

[129] Associated Press. "Israel's Inflation Rate Down to Zero in July." *Los Angeles Times*, 17 August 1986, www.latimes.com/archives/la-xpm-1986-08-17-mn-16602-story.html

[130] "Silicon Valley to Silicon Wadi: California's Economic Ties with Israel." *Bay Area Council Economic Institute*, October 2021, www.bayareaeconomy.org/report/silicon-valley-to-silicon-wadi/

[131] Senor, Dan and Saul Singer. (2011). *Start-up Nation: The Story of Israel's Economic Miracle*. Twelve. www.amazon.com/Start-up-Nation-Israels-Economic-Miracle/dp/0446541478/ref=nodl_?dplnkId=868ab204-c8f8-4247-9e3e-53022b3e6ea8

motive and mobility industries. According to a McKinsey report,[132] the market for automotive software and electronics may become a $470 billion industry by 2030.

The image of a people on the move, of the children of G-d and the sons of Abraham working in peace, at peace with the parties to the Abraham Accords,[133] is no illusion. And the image of a people enriching their nation by increasing the wealth of all free nations—an image of peace and prosperity—is no fantasy.

The image is true.

*

"Viewing this strange and singular history one cannot escape the impression that it must contain some special significance for the history of mankind, that in some way, whether one believes in divine purpose or inscrutable circumstance, the Jews have been singled out to carry the tale of human fate."

—Barbara W. Tuchman, *Bible and Sword: England and Palestine from the Bronze Age to Balfour*

So long as the Jewish people carry Israel with them, the children of Israel will have the freedom to carry on the tale of the Jewish people. And if the Jewish people choose to carry the tale, chosenness will be a high honor and a hard duty to honor, for nothing about the tale involves power or privilege.

---

132 Maor et al. "Israel: Hot spot for future mobility technologies." *McKinsey & Company*, 18 September 2019, www.mckinsey.com/industries/automotive-and-assembly/our-insights/israel-hot-spot-for-future-mobility-technologies

133 "The Abraham Accords." *U.S. Department of State*, 15 September 2020, www.state.gov/the-abraham-accords/

Chosenness is a tale of rites, not rights to do as one pleases. For the tale would not exist without the righteous among the nations in which the Jews live.

The tale of human fate is what we make of it. For while we talk of many things, a King[134] of a preacher adds his word to what we have said. He says, "All men are caught in an inescapable network of mutuality, tied in a single garment of destiny. Whatever affects one directly, affects all indirectly."

Yet, if destiny wills men to tear the garment and dip it in blood, and sin upon their father's favorite son, and sell their own brother into slavery, the dream of Israel shall not die.

The soul of Israel, like the spirit of all great nations, is indestructible.

The defense of the Jewish state shows that Israel is like a rock that provides shelter from the wind and refuge from the storm. And from this rock comes water, like rivers in the desert and salvation in a weary land.

The life of Israel belongs to the ages.

---

[134] King, Martin Luther Jr. "Letter from Birmingham Jail." *The Martin Luther King, Jr. Research and Education Institute*, 16 April 1963, https://kinginstitute.stanford.edu/sites/mlk/files/letterfrombirmingham_wwcw_0.pdf

CHAPTER 5

New Money

"Cryptocurrency currencies take the concept of money, and they take it native into computers, where everything is settled with computers and doesn't require external institutions or trusted third parties to validate things."

—Naval Ravikant, entrepreneur and investor

The total face value of Washington, Jefferson, Hamilton, Jackson, Lincoln, and Grant is $88.

The faces denote different values, just as the faces represent men of different and conflicting values. In them we see the Father of the Nation and the founder of the Democratic-Republican Party. We see the Founding Father and father of the Federalist Party and the father of the Democratic Party. We see the greatest president since Washington and the first Republican since Lincoln to serve as president.

Add Franklin to the equation and the total is $188.

The names belong to the faces on money, with Franklin more popular than all except Washington, and Jefferson least popular of all.

But the names, age, and faces fade before their time—not because of how much money trades hands, but because of how much less paper money[135] we carry and touch with our own hands. And because of how much less currency of a certain kind we possess, in terms of knowledge of the values of great men.

We owe it to ourselves and our posterity to preserve the wealth of knowledge of and about our nation, stockpiling one form of currency as we use new currencies. The sources are several and the materials many, resulting in a resource with more intelligence than the Library of Congress and more information than all past House and Senate Select Committees on Intelligence combined.

The resource is a smartphone, one of 6.6 billion such devices, with which people read and write and text in lieu of writing, all while sending over $700 billion[136] in remittances each year.

The work of foreign workers—be they guest workers or migrant workers, both in the fields and in the streets—is the work of nations. And the money these workers earn abroad is the bulk of the money they transfer home, uniting workers of the world through remittances to India, China, Mexico, the Philippines, Egypt, Lebanon, and Honduras.

But the cost of these transfers is more onerous than the labors these workers perform. This cost is unacceptable, exacting a separate and unequal tax on weeks and months of toil until the little these workers have is everything financial institutions consume.

Workers are right to reject this cost. They can apply their collective strength not to the promotion of collectivism but the protec-

---

[135] Dickler, Jessica. "More Americans say they don't carry cash." CNBC, 15 January 2019, www.cnbc.com/2019/01/15/more-americans-say-they-dont-carry-cash.html

[136] McCarthy, Niall. "These countries are the world's top remittance recipients." *World Economic Forum*, 19 May 2021, www.weforum.org/agenda/2021/05/infographic-what-are-the-world-s-top-remittance-recipients/

tion of capitalism. And they are right to save capitalism from the enemies of free and fair markets—thanks to an ongoing revolution in finance.

The revolution is real. It is observable and accessible in real time thanks to the radicalism of transparency and the triumph of technology.

Thanks to blockchain technology, a peer-to-peer network that time-stamps and secures every transaction, workers can make haste, not waste. They can send or receive money free of delays. And they can deny banks and financial institutions the freedom to delay the transfer of funds, or the opportunity to make money—to accrue interest—free of charge, while the poor pay for nothing and the needy get nothing in return.

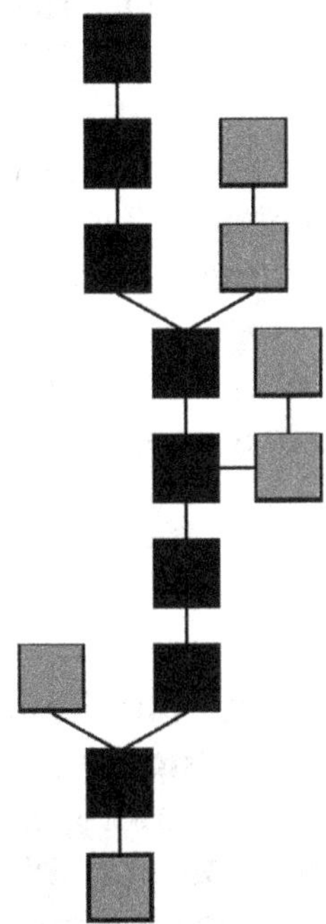

Without this technology, no celebration of the working man can allay the pain workers fear. No fanfare for the common man can ease the pain workers feel. And no worker can end the economic pain his fellow man endures.

With this technology, workers can remit more money with lower fees. In fact, they can remit however much money they want—regardless of the type of money they choose to send—for a standard fee of one percent.

This advantage redounds to my benefit, too, because I am an investor in a blockchain-based platform for fast and secure transfers and quantum-proof digital vaulting of fiat currencies and cryptocurrencies.

I mention my investment for two reasons. First, I believe in radical transparency and personal integrity. Second, I insist that people see for themselves what neo-banking offers, rather than taking my word for it. After all, it's wrong to trust what I say without first confirming that what I say is true.

About the nomenclature of remittances (which is a fancy way of saying how financial institutions word or name things), the next chapter defines a variety of relevant topics.

About the things banks and financial services companies do to shortchange consumers, this chapter explains why things must change.

*

"To understand the evolution of bank design, it is also necessary to grasp the fundamentals of America's banking and financial history, which go hand-in-hand with the creation of bank architecture."

—Charles Belfoure, *Monuments to Money*

For 1.7 billion people around the world, a passbook[137] is another word for a passport, while a Christmas club[138] is what it sounds like.

Were we to ask people about the two, would they say the former is a prerequisite for the latter? Would they say a passbook opens the membership book of a Christmas club? Or would they say one is for personal banking and the other a bank promotion?

They would say they do not have a passbook—regardless of their interest in a Christmas club—because none of them has a bank account.

For a group seven times larger than the median asset size of a bank[139] in the United States, and four points shy of a quarter of the world's population, a bank account[140] is a foreign concept. And for these people, the passbook is no scrapbook. Billions do not recognize what millions will never see again: monuments to money.

None shall pass through the bronze doors or see the symbols of prosperity. They will not witness the images shining as horns of plenty, the doors that open into a hanging garden of chandeliers with glass and gold trimmings, the teller windows with their copper bars and marble inserts, or the vault door that reveals a wall of steel and a row of safe deposit boxes.

---

137 "Vintage Bank of America Savings Account Passbook." *WorthPoint*, 1953, www.worthpoint.com/worthopedia/vintage-bank-america-savings-account-469899289

138 "Vintage Christmas Club Banking Sealed Packet Book—State Bank Fayetteville, TN." *WorthPoint*, www.worthpoint.com/worthopedia/vintage-christmas-club-banking-sealed-1907613451

139 "Biggest U.S. Banks by Asset Size." *MX Blog*, 20 April 2021, www.mx.com/blog/biggest-banks-by-asset-size-united-states/

140 "Gains in Financial Inclusion, Gains for a Sustainable World." *The World Bank*, 18 May 2016, www.worldbank.org/en/news/immersive-story/2018/05/18/gains-in-financial-inclusion-gains-for-a-sustainable-world

Today, people pass through the doors of the mundane. They stand in line like travelers at an airport. They linger beneath fluorescent lights like ceiling pipes, in a space with concrete walls and plastic chairs. They stand inside a money transfer location, in need of help.

The best way to help these people is to let them keep more of their money. And the fastest way to make help available is through blockchain technology.

That people should avail themselves of this opportunity, migrating from Western Union or MoneyGram to a solution like VeroWay[141], is critical. For the more than 270 million[142] migrants who send remittances in a given year, mass migration to the blockchain is key.

The key is one of a pair, with the two freeing bodies and minds. For the freedom to move money is the freedom to take a giant leap. It is the freedom to step out of line and leave a money transfer location for good.

But freedom of action is nothing without freedom of information. Someone who does not know why he should move will stand in line until he leaves a money transfer location with less of his own money. Understanding how money transfer firms work—that these firms risk nothing while rewarding only themselves—is key to this discussion.

For example, according to Stephen Cecchetti, Rosen Family Chair in International Finance at Brandeis International Business School, and Kim Schoenholtz, Henry Kaufman Professor of the History of Financial Institutions and Markets at NYU Stern School of Business,

---

141 "VeroWay Group Introduction." *VeroWay*, 2023, www.veroway.com

142 McAuliffe, Marie and Binod Khadria. "Providing Perspective on Migration and Mobility in Increasingly Uncertain Times." *World Migration Report 2020*, https://publications.iom.int/system/files/pdf/wmr_2020_en_Chapter1_004.pdf

the charge[143] for sending $200—the benchmark authorities use to measure cost—is $14. That equates to 7 percent of the money sent,

This charge is close to the average stock market return over the last twenty years[144]—*before* accounting for inflation.

Adjusted for inflation, the market's performance falls from 7.45 percent to 5.3 percent.

No wonder money transfer firms do well, with MoneyGram[145] charging $12.50 for a domestic transfer of $200 in cash and Western Union[146] charging $17.50 for the same transaction.

*

"Financial illiteracy is not an issue unique to any one population. It affects everyone: men and women, young and old, across all racial and socioeconomic lines. No longer can we stand by and ignore this problem. The economic future of the United States depends on it."

—President's Advisory Council on Financial Literacy

According to a report[147]commissioned by TransferWire and published by Capital Economics, Americans paid $16.3 billion in fees on remittances and international payments in a single year. The report also says Americans overpaid by more than half, due to $8.7 billion in hidden and inflated exchange rates.

---

143 Schoenholtz, Kim and Stephen Cecchetti. "The stubbornly high cost of remittances." *VoxEU*, 27 March 2018, https://cepr.org/voxeu/columns/stubbornly-high-cost-remittances

144 Lake, Rebecca. "What Is the Average Stock Market Return?" *SoFi*, 28 December 2022, www.sofi.com/learn/content/average-stock-market-return/

145 "Rates & Fees." *MoneyGram*, www.moneygram.com/mgo/us/en/

146 "Send Money Online." *Western Union*, www.westernunion.com/us/en/web/send-money/start

147 "Estimating the scale of foreign exchange transaction fees in the U.S." *Capital Economics*, https://wise.com/documents/Public_Research_and_Survey_-_US_Hidden_Fees.pdf

An overpayment that large is a tax—a financial literacy tax—that weakens our will and degrades our humanity. This tax demands redress in law and recognition through a presidential address to the nation, thus forging the promise of freedom with the reality of opportunity and meting out justice for a just and lasting peace between friends, not enemies. For we must never again be enemies. We must meet in the middle as Americans, Democrats and Republicans, in the spirit of Lyndon Johnson's decision to finish the work of Abraham Lincoln, instead of repeating the sins of Andrew Johnson. We must adhere to Johnson's saying[148]:

The central fact of American civilization—one so hard for others to understand—is that freedom and justice and the dignity of man are not just words to us. We believe in them. Under all the growth and the tumult and abundance, we believe. And so, as long as some among us are oppressed—and we are part of that oppression—it must blunt our faith and sap the strength of our high purpose.

Words of high purpose are clear. And yet words alone will not repeal the fees Americans pay, especially if the words are extraneous and do not itemize—and explain—every fee a consumer must pay.

About one word in particular, whose purpose is invaluable and whose absence is obvious, the world's largest organizations—

---

[148] Johnson, Lyndon B. "Remarks on the Signing of the Voting Rights Act." *Miller Center*, 6 August 1965, https://millercenter.org/the-presidency/presidential-speeches/august-6-1965-remarks-signing-voting-rights-act

from the United Nations[149] to the World Bank[150] to the World Economic Forum[151]—agree.

The word is "transparency."

My definition of the word is a quality or state, the state (in this case) being a series of statements involving remittances, freedom of information, and the underpinnings of a free market.

According to *Remittance Prices Worldwide*[152], which provides data on the cost of sending and receiving small amounts of money from one country to another, consumers cannot compare what they cannot see. And due to a lack of transparency, they cannot compare costs.

Publicity will not reduce this problem. And negative publicity will not remedy this problem. The *system* is the problem. It is profitable because it is inefficient, with no motive to police itself save one: self-preservation.

The system seeks to save itself, even if the price of success is the evisceration of the poor and the impoverishment of the working class.

---

149 Antunes, Bruno. "Financial Inclusion: Better Access to Financial Services for Women, the Poor, and Migrant Work." *United Nations Conference on Trade and Development (UNCTAD)*, 2021 https://unctad.org/system/files/official-document/ditctncd2020d6_en.pdf

150 Käärmann, Kristo."Ending remittance hidden fees: the international community calls for action." *World Bank Blogs*, 5 May 2021, https://blogs.worldbank.org/peoplemove/ending-remittance-hidden-fees-international-community-calls-action

151 Ratha, Dilip. "Why we need to cut remittance fees now." *World Economic Forum*, 4 March 2015, www.weforum.org/agenda/2015/03/why-we-need-to-cut-remittance-fees-now/

152 "Remittance Prices Worldwide." *The World Bank*, https://remittanceprices.worldbank.org/about-remittance-prices-worldwide

The system's use of wealth stripping is the economic equivalent of strip mining, which causes visible and lasting harm to the environment. Like a gash in the earth, spilling debris and scattering dust, the harm cannot heal without scarring. The scars rank in rows, exposing the slums and shanty towns—ridges upon ridges—of the underclass.

The harm deepens in Asia and deteriorates throughout Africa and the Americas. Meanwhile, U.N. Secretary-General Antonio Guterres[153] calls for remittance fees to be set "as close to zero as possible," and for those in the industry to "foster the financial inclusion of migrants and their families."

One percent is as close to zero as possible. And it is possible today—through blockchain based digital money transfer platforms. I have invested in some of them and will continue to seek out new opportunities in this exciting decentralized finance world.

One percent fees for money transfers benefit all people, 99 percent of whom occupy tax brackets far below the top-earning one percent. Without this alternative, zero has a different and more ominous meaning. And without any alternative, wealth stripping will leave many with nothing.

So says the Institute for Policy Studies[154], which predicts that the median Black household will have zero wealth by 2053. The same report says the median Latino household wealth will hit zero in twenty years.

---

[153] "UN Calls for Better Remittance Services at Lower Cost." *VOA*, 16 June 2021, www.voanews.com/a/usa_un-calls-better-remittance-services-lower-cost/6207083.html

[154] Collins et al. "Report: The Road to Zero Wealth." *Institute for Policy Studies*, 11 September 2017, https://ips-dc.org/report-the-road-to-zero-wealth/

Another report—this one from Global Market Insights[155] (GMI)—estimates digital-only banking will have a compound annual growth rate of 45 percent between now and 2028, or a market size greater than $600 billion.

Not every prediction is prophetic. We have it in our power to begin the financial world over again. With blockchain technology specifically, we have the power to begin again. We can make every fee transparent and every transaction easy to see.

A new chapter in finance awaits us, beginning with the details in the next chapter.

155 "Neobanking Market." *Global Market Insights (GMI)*, February 2022, www.gminsights.com/industry-analysis/neobanking-market

CHAPTER 6
The Details

"It doesn't matter if you're a hedge fund manager on Wall Street or if you're one of the 1.7 billion people that don't even have a bank account. With DeFi, you have complete access."
—Rune Christiansen, CEO of the Maker Foundation

Decentralized finance (DeFi) is the antithesis of the financial establishment. It is free of the controls—including those governing the free flow of information—that favor institutions over individual investors.

DeFi returns power to the people, giving each person the right to see and manage his own money. With this freedom comes choice. You have the right to choose the market of trade, the medium of exchange, the products to trade, and the currencies for trading. All this culminates in a transparent and secure trading system.

Trading does not stop with the ringing of a bell. For there are no bells to ring or hours to follow, or holidays to observe or days in which banking goes on holiday. Access requires nothing more than an internet connection.

Take, for instance, how citizens in Argentina[156] and Brazil[157] use DeFi to hedge inflation and access the crypto economy. About the latter, think of Bitcoin as the first DeFi application. Regardless of what one thinks of Bitcoin or cryptocurrencies in general, the issue is real and the market is rich.

Because the market is also volatile, caution is necessary.

Caution is a warning, as clear in words as it is visible in works. It is an upraised hand—a symbol of order—rather than belief in the orderliness of the invisible hand.

*

"If the cryptocurrency market overall or a digital asset is solving a problem, it's going to drive some value."
—Brad Garlinghouse, CEO of Ripple Labs

What attracts value does not a priori repel volatility.

Put another way, markets fluctuate, and volatile markets fluctuate wildly. The price of Bitcoin reflects this fact.

---

[156] Goschenko, Sergio. "Brazil and Argentina Present in Chainalysis Defi Adoption Index." *Bitcoin.com News*, 26 August 2021, https://news.bitcoin.com/brazil-and-argentina-present-in-chainalysis-defi-adoption-index/

[157] Majcher, Kristin. "DeFi ETFs take flight in Brazil with two launches this month." *The Block*, 17 February 2022, www.theblock.co/linked/134662/defi-etfs-take-flight-in-brazil-with-two-launches-this-month

But volatility is not an accurate measure of utility, because the value a good provides is not always commensurate with value-based pricing. I believe this assertion is true of most goods. And it is true for Bitcoin, regardless of what others believe.

Some critics believe Bitcoin is a scheme, while Bitcoin maximalists believe fiat money is a con. But I accept Bitcoin for what it is: a reality.

As for Satoshi Nakamoto[158], the pseudonymous inventor of Bitcoin and the first blockchain, I believe no man is above the law of unintended consequences and no man is below it.

That is to say, Nakamoto's argument for Bitcoin is a vision that does not envision problems of its own. What he says on paper, in his white paper (*Bitcoin: A Peer-to-Peer Electronic Cash System*[159]), is clear. And much of what he says about conventional currencies and central banks is true.

But what he says in the last sentence of his section on incentive is not the last word—far from it—on mining Bitcoin: "The steady addition of a constant of [*sic*] amount of new coins is analogous to gold miners expending resources to add gold to circulation. In our case, it is CPU time and electricity that is expended."

By not assigning numbers to time and power, Nakamoto excludes the rates at which the energy efficiency and processing power of computers double. Not that it matters, because the combination

---

[158] "History." *Satoshi Nakamoto Institute*, https://nakamotoinstitute.org/about/

[159] Nakamoto, Satoshi. "Bitcoin: A Peer-to-Peer Electronic Cash System." *Bitcoin.org*, 31 October 2008, https://bitcoin.org/bitcoin.pdf

of Koomey's Law[160] and Moore's Law[161] makes the theory of mining Bitcoin seem overly optimistic.

Along with electricity, which seems incidental, Nakamoto's theory sounds like an irresistible incentive to accumulate gold. Never mind that the steady addition of new coins is *not* analogous to adding gold, because the amount of minable Bitcoin is definite while the amount of gold still to be mined is indeterminate.

Bear in mind, too, that criticism—factual criticism—is not proof of a fatal flaw.

But the unintended consequence of CPU time and electricity is a sum separate from the expenditure of resources. This sum, unknown or unknowable at the start, is now undeniable.

According to Cambridge University's Bitcoin Electricity Consumption Index[162], the sum total of Bitcoin mining exceeds the annual energy usage of Norway and is close to the annual energy budget of Argentina. And in the United States alone, Bitcoin mining produces an estimated 40 billion pounds[163] of carbon dioxide per year.

In response to these facts, Tesla made it more difficult for consumers to use most cryptocurrencies to buy their cars. Tesla CEO

---

[160] Yirka, Bob. 15 September 2011, "New 'Koomey's Law' of power efficiency parallels Moore's Law." *Phys.org*, https://phys.org/news/2011-09-koomeys-law-power-efficiency-parallels.html

[161] Kelleher, Ann. "Moore's Law—Now and in the Future." *Intel*, 16 February 2022, https://download.intel.com/newsroom/2022/manufacturing/Intel-Moores-Law-Investor-Meeting-Paper-final.pdf

[162] "Bitcoin network power demand." *Cambridge Centre for Alternative Finance*, https://ccaf.io/cbeci/index/comparisons

[163] Kim, Paul. "What are the environmental impacts of cryptocurrencies?" *Business Insider*, 17 March 2022, www.businessinsider.com/personal-finance/cryptocurrency-environmental-impact

Elon Musk[164] said, "Cryptocurrency is a good idea on many levels and we believe it has a promising future, but this cannot come at great cost to the environment."

My response is to state the facts.

Where the facts speak for themselves, I repeat them. Where the facts speak of different things, I translate them. Where the facts speak to differences among things, I interpret them.

My interpretation of the responses and counter-responses is that Musk is a realist while Nakamoto is an idealist. I believe the former is right about the idea of cryptocurrency while the latter is wrong not to consider the degree of resistance to his ideas.

Take, for instance, Nakamoto's statement[165] about the root problem with conventional currency—that it cannot work without trust:

The central bank must be trusted not to debase the currency, but the history of fiat currencies is full of breaches of that trust. Banks must be trusted to hold our money and transfer it electronically, but they lend it out in waves of credit bubbles with barely a fraction in reserve. We have to trust them with our privacy, trust them not to let identity thieves drain our accounts.

---

[164] Musk, E. [@elonmusk]. (2021, May 12). Tesla has suspended vehicle purchases using Bitcoin. We are concerned about rapidly increasing use of fossil fuels for Bitcoin mining and transactions, especially coal, which has the worst emissions of any fuel. Cryptocurrency is a good idea on many levels and we believe it has a promising future, but this cannot come at great cost to the environment. Tesla will not be selling any Bitcoin and we intend to use it for transactions as soon as mining transitions to more sustainable energy. We are also looking at other cryptocurrencies that use <1% of Bitcoin's energy/transaction. [Tweet]. Twitter. https://twitter.com/elonmusk/status/1392602041025843203?s=46&t=Iqlu26AH1LJzdIukLL_tyQ

[165] Nakamoto, Satoshi. "Bitcoin open source implementation of P2P currency." *Satoshi Nakamoto Institute*, 2 November 2009, https://satoshi.nakamotoinstitute.org/posts/p2pfoundation/1/

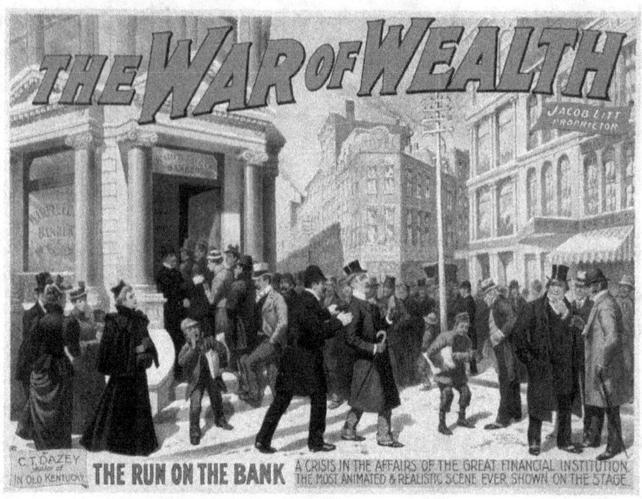

Trust is rare, as the history of trusts in America proves and as America's response to the rise of trusts demonstrates, with Theodore Roosevelt[166] denouncing the anarchist who preaches violence—he who inveighs against wealth—and malefactors of great wealth.

Trust runs from the sound of fear.

The sound travels from the recent past to the distant past, from the Great Recession to the Great Depression to the first Bank War. It passes from George W. Bush to George H.W. Bush, from the age of Franklin D. Roosevelt to the age of Andrew Jackson. It's a powerful sound, one that makes the White House complex a stage, from the Cabinet Room to the Diplomatic Reception Room to the Oval Office. It's a crescendo of rhetoric ending in the passage of laws and the passing of pens, regardless of what a president says.

---

166 Roosevelt, Theodore. "First Annual Message." *The American Presidency Project*, 3 December 1901, www.presidency.ucsb.edu/documents/first-annual-message-16

Whether Ronald Reagan[167] speaks of expanding the powers of thrift institutions and empowering institutions to act like spendthrifts, or H.W. Bush[168] signs legislation to rescue the thrifts, the sound is the same. And so too is the result. It stays the same when Reagan speaks of his hope for more of the same, of repealing the Glass-Steagall Act,[169] or when a Democrat strikes a deal with Republicans and repeals the Act, or when the president is a former Democrat or a New Democrat.

Whether the Act speaks to the coming of the New Deal and passage of the Banking Act of 1933—or the Act ends with the Gramm-Leach-Bliley Act[170]—and whether FDR speaks of salvation[171] for some banks or Bill Clinton[172] speaks of granting more authority for all banks, the reality is also the same.

[167] Reagan, Ronald. "Remarks on Signing the Garn-St Germain Depository Institutions Act of 1982." *Ronald Reagan Presidential Library & Museum*, 15 October 1982, www.reaganlibrary.gov/archives/speech/remarks-signing-garn-st-germain-depository-institutions-act-1982

[168] "Savings & Loan Legislation Signing Ceremony." *C-SPAN*, 9 August 1989, www.c-span.org/video/?8653-1/savings-loan-legislation-signing-ceremony

[169] "Banking Act of 1933 (Glass-Steagall Act)." *Federal Reserve Bank of St. Louis*, 16 June 1933, https://fraser.stlouisfed.org/title/banking-act-1933-glass-steagall-act-991

[170] "S.900 - Gramm-Leach-Bliley Act." *Congress.gov*, 12 November 1999, www.congress.gov/bill/106th-congress/senate-bill/900

[171] Roosevelt, Franklin D. "Fireside Chat 1: On the Banking Crisis." *Miller Center*, 12 March 1933, https://millercenter.org/the-presidency/presidential-speeches/march-12-1933-fireside-chat-1-banking-crisis

[172] "Financial Services Bill Signing." *C-SPAN*, 12 November 1999, www.c-span.org/video/?153587-1/financial-services-bill-signing

The reality of betrayal starts with trust—from the sins of the first man to suffering for the sins of all men, from the father of humanity to the Son of the Father.

Betrayal abounds in the books of history and the holy books. Nakamoto says as much in his own way, focusing on the nature of one problem without considering the broader problem of human nature.

He overlooks the fact that imperfection—the fallibility of man—is inherent in any system. He overlooks that the code by which a system runs or the code of conduct that keeps a system running is not immune to error.

To wit, cryptocurrency-based crime is a $14 billion[173] phenomenon, up 79 percent from $7.8 billion in 2020.

That the Bitcoin white paper says nothing about crypto crime is understandable. Looking back on 2008, between the release of the white paper and the results on the night of Election Day—a total of four days—the immediate future looked bad. The near future looked bleak, and the not-too-distant future blank.

With time comes perspective and the context to view the past without conscious bias. Within the larger context of cryptocurrency transactions, $14 billion in illicit transactions represents 0.15 percent of all transaction volume in 2021. In comparison, $15.8 trillion[174] in transaction volume represents a 567 percent increase in the trading of digital assets.

---

173 Chavez-Dreyfuss, Gertrude. "Cryptocurrency crime in 2021 hits all-time high in value—Chainanlysis." *Reuters*, 6 January 2022, www.reuters.com/markets/us/cryptocurrency-crime-2021-hits-all-time-high-value-chainalysis-2022-01-06/

174 Chainalysis team. "Crypto Crime Trends for 2022: Illicit Transaction Activity Reaches All-Time High in Value, All-Time Low in Share of All Cryptocurrency Activity." *Chainalysis*, 6 January 2022, https://blog.chainalysis.com/reports/2022-crypto-crime-report-introduction/

Without this comparison, numbers have no context. And because of this comparison, the Bitcoin white paper adds context to this discussion.

Given the context at the time—between the hazards of the economy and the moral hazards of economic policy, and with governments and central banks picking winners and losers—the white paper is a product of its time.

Looking back on this time, what looks novel is the novelty of the white paper itself.

That the white paper reads like a novel, in the sense that it proposes the creation of a virtual currency independent of the banking system, is no different than any other proposal that seems impossible.

Time changes how certain opportunities look. And my outlook changes regarding which investment opportunities look best.

Again, I look at $15.8 trillion in transaction volume as a reality too big to ignore.

Aware of the reality of this situation—and with awareness of the unintended consequences of this situation—I also see the unexpected benefits. Among these are a multiplicity of systems and coins, and one overarching system of decentralized finance, resulting in lower transaction fees and a ledger of all transactions.

I see advances in computing and strides (however small) toward quantum computing[175], resulting in the expansion of the

---

[175] Singer, Andrew. "Quantum computing to run economic models on crypto adoption." *Cointelegraph*, 22 April 2022, https://cointelegraph.com/news/quantum-computing-to-run-economic-models-on-crypto-adoption

metaverse[176] and variations[177] of the metaverse. And I see these things within the context of access and choice, the two increasing through fractional ownership of digital assets.

People can buy Bitcoin and other cryptocurrencies for less than a dollar, executing trades via financial apps, exchanges, trading apps, or traditional brokers. Or they can buy non-fungible tokens (NFTs) containing references to digital files such as art, music, videos, and photographs.

People can achieve a lot and buy many precious things with crypto. But the last thing anyone should do is buy crypto on trust alone. Trusting that something is what someone else says it is, that an investment is safe or a stablecoin stable, is an intolerable risk.

*

"Because he could not afford to fail, he could not afford to trust."

—Joseph J. Ellis,
His Excellency: George Washington

Trust no one to protect what you cannot afford to lose.

Trust that nothing is as it seems, especially when someone appropriates the symbols of trust and faces criminal charges involving the misappropriation of customer funds.

---

176 Ravenscraft, Eric. "What Is the Metaverse, Exactly?" *Wired*, 25 April 2022, www.wired.com/story/what-is-the-metaverse/

177 Gurau, Michael, "A Multiverse Of Metaverses." *Forbes*, 22 March 2022, www.forbes.com/sites/forbestechcouncil/2022/03/22/a-multiverse-of-metaverses/

Trust that Sam Bankman-Fried (SBF[178]), founder and CEO of cryptocurrency exchange FTX, is in a lot of trouble.

If the charges against SBF are true, know that trust is an ineffective check on the machinations of an advocate of effective altruism[179]. The appurtenances of wealth do not make investors wealthy, just as the accouterments of power do not make investors powerful.

If SBF is guilty of wire fraud, wire fraud conspiracy, securities fraud, securities fraud conspiracy, and money laundering, know that trust is no substitute for transparency.

If SBF's investors feel guilty—if they regret their losses and rue their decision to give him their money—they now know the perils of trust.

*

"But it has not been for nothing that the word has remained man's principal toy and tool: without the meanings and values it sustains, all man's other tools would be worthless."

—Lewis Mumford,
The Transformation of Man

When the worth of a word fluctuates, or the meaning of a word that denotes little or no fluctuation becomes worthless, the values that sustain us disappear.

---

178 Schwartz, Brian. "Sam Bankman-Fried diverted FTX customer funds to donate to political campaigns, authorities charge." *CNBC*, 13 December 2022, www.cnbc.com/amp/2022/12/13/ftx-founder-sam-bankman-fried-charged-with-campaign-finance-violations-in-criminal-indictment.html

179 Levitz, Eric. "Is Effective Altruism to Blame for Sam Bankman-Fried?" *New York*, 16 November 2022, https://nymag.com/intelligencer/2022/11/effective-altruism-sam-bankman-fried-sbf-ftx-crypto.html

When a word can no longer sustain the worth of a good, a sell-off will occur.

When the good is an algorithmic stablecoin—a coin backed not by assets but by assertions in the form of equations—and when the coin in question has a fixed price and its sister token does not, differences in price can trigger a massive sell-off.

The collapse of TerraUSD[180] (UST) proves this point. An offshoot of Luna, a cryptocurrency on the Terra blockchain, UST lost 70 percent of its value when Luna fell. The problem was that the stability of UST depended on the sustainability of Luna, which meant Luna had to attract stakeholders. To accomplish this, Luna offered a 19.5 percent yield on staking.

This return was—surprise—unsustainable.

When Duo Nine[181], a cryptocurrency analyst, said there were not enough reserves to meet the yield and that all reserves would hit zero within twenty days, Do Kwon[182], co-founder of Terraform Labs, said things were fine. And then on May 16, 2022, four months and eleven days after Kwon said any such situation was hypothetical, the price of UST was nine cents.

---

180 Browne, Ryan. "$3 billion in bitcoin was sold in a last-ditch attempt to save UST stablecoin from collapse." *CNBC*, 16 May 2022, www.cnbc.com/amp/2022/05/16/what-happened-to-the-bitcoin-reserve-behind-terras-ust-stablecoin.html

181 Godbole, Omkar. "Anchor Protocol Reserves Slide as Money Market's Founder Talks Down Concerns." *CoinDesk*, 28 January 2022, www.coindesk.com/markets/2022/01/28/anchor-protocol-reserves-slide-as-money-markets-founder-talks-down-concerns/

182 Kwon, D. [@stablekwon]. (2022, January 27). 7/ ... and with staking returns + ANC borrowing incentives it will still offer a rate of 15-16%. If we were to get to this hypothetical situation, Anchor will *still* offer the highest ra return on stablecoins. By far. It will be fine. [Tweet]. Twitter. https://twitter.com/stablekwon/status/1486878321245708289?s=46&t=7z2BDgBH_yogBtIN7u88mA

To call this outcome a black swan[183] event is to ignore the evidence.

To criticize the critics who demand evidence, who say, "Do your own research (DYOR)," is to replace truth with trust. Or so the *New York Times*[184] implies.

Trust that the *Times* is wrong about trust.

*

"Only those you trust can betray you."
—Terry Goodkind, *Stone of Tears*

Picture CNBC running promos[185] with the tagline "In Cramer We Trust."

Picture the promos running at a time when Jim Cramer, the host of *Mad Money*[186] and the supposed expert in whom CNBC trusts, faces a crisis of confidence as banks face a liquidity crisis. This as his recommendations, and the exuberance with which he issues

---

[183] Qureshi, Mehab. "The great Luna-Terra crash: 5 lessons to be learned." *Indian Express*, 5 June 2022, https://indianexpress.com/article/technology/crypto/the-great-luna-terra-2-0-crash-5-lessons-to-be-learned-7947848/

[184] Herrman, John. "They Did Their Own 'Research.' Now What?" *New York Times*, 29 May 2022, www.nytimes.com/2022/05/29/style/do-your-own-research.html?smid=nytcore-ios-sharehttps://www.nytimes.com/2022/05/29/style/do-your-own-research.html?referringSource=articleShare

[185] CNBC Prime. (2008, October 15). *In Cramer We Trust* [Video]. YouTube. https://youtu.be/U3EulyICWFc

[186] Mad Money on CNBC. [@MadMoneyOnCNBC]. (2017, November 20). .@JimCramer's rolling up his sleeves to give his hot take on $OLED [Tweet]. Twitter. https://twitter.com/madmoneyoncnbc/status/932700089541259265?s=46&t=UQ1b07InxBFCZgd7-AeIlg

them, face mockery[187] and scorn[188]. This as his recommendations stop generating positive returns.

Picture the flow of hot air through a cool medium, a collision of styles resulting in a front of confusion, where the personality on-screen dresses for radio but appears on TV. And if that picture shows Jim Cramer[189] rolling up his sleeves, picture *Network*[190] as a documentary and *Talk Radio*[191] as reality TV.

The picture does not inspire trust. No—it calls attention to itself. And that's the point. Because nothing on TV—not even commercial-free programming—is free. Every show has a sponsor because every show has something to sell. Even if there were no sponsorship rules or on-air disclosures, the hard sell of the pledge drive would prevail.

All shows would be one show: a telethon of improvisation and despair, where attention must be paid to the person on-screen.

---

[187] The Daily Show Episode: In Cramer We Trust [Video]. Retrieved from Comedy Central: https://www.cc.com/video/m0dbcb/the-daily-show-with-jon-stewart-in-cramer-we-trust

[188] "Stewart vs. Jim Cramer." *New York Times*, 4 August 2015, www.nytimes.com/video/arts/television/100000003836291/stewart-vs-jim-cramer.html?smid=nytcore-ios-share

[189] Twitter Post: [@MadMoneyOnCNBC]. (2017, November 20). Inverted yield curve leads to new market highs... [Tweet]. Retrieved from https://twitter.com/madmoneyoncnbc/status/932700089541259265?

[190] *Network—Trailer.* Directed by Sidney Lumet, performances by Peter Finch, Robert Duvall, Faye Dunaway, and William Holden, Warner Bros., 1976. YouTube, uploaded by Warner Bros., 8 July 2014 https://youtu.be/xxajGBZeQZc

[191] *Talk Radio—Preview.* Directed by Oliver Stone, performances by Eric Bogosian, Alec Baldwin, Ellen Greene, Leslie Hope, and John C. McGinley, Universal Pictures, 1988. YouTube, uploaded by YouTube Movies & TV, https://youtu.be/5p-9Ut4g3xw

(The line about attention is from *Death of a Salesman*[192]. It is the antithesis of a sales pitch. The line is a *cri de coeur* on the degradation of a man and the planned obliteration of all mankind.)

Even when the pitch is soft, airing after the end of the trading week and replicating the ringing of the trading bell, the show continues to sell. Even when the pitchman is dead, it sells.

Watch any episode of *Wall Street Week with Louis Rukeyser*[193], whose boardroom-in-a-penthouse style looks like *Playboy's Penthouse*[194] for investors, and the selling is unmistakable.

As for the views and opinions expressed by Rukeyser and his guests—they do not necessarily reflect an investment philosophy. These views must have a basis in fact, or all the facts must fit together, lest people differ over what the facts mean. And the show must present an accurate representation of reality, otherwise the opinions expressed are no different than the naming of shadows.

Unless viewers understand that assertiveness does not prove an assertion, the person on-screen—the person with the loudest voice but the weakest case—will continue to influence how people invest.

*

[192] *Death of a Salesman*. Directed by László Benedek, performances by Mildred Dunnock and Kevin McCarthy, Columbia Pictures, 1951. YouTube, uploaded by Bob Foreman, 1 May 2021 https://youtu.be/fmjsubPVB14

[193] crashof1987. (2016, May 20). *Wall Street Week with Louis Rukeyser* [Video]. YouTube. https://youtu.be/i9GsilQ6jUc

[194] AZIA Black. (2017, November 26). *Playboy's Penthouse Season 1 Episode 17 ft. Tony Bennett, Phyllis Diller, Joe Williams* [Video]. YouTube. https://youtu.be/E8vMJqmAuNs

"Arbitrage will take place whenever there is an imbalance created in one or more markets that are similar."
—John Gutfreund, former CEO of Salomon Brothers

Where difference reveals imbalance, opportunity exists.

Where language fails to conceal imbalance, evidence of opportunity exists.

Where traders see an opportunity to profit from imbalance, arbitrage exists.

Seizing an opportunity is a separate matter, made easier by proof of an obvious and unsustainable imbalance in pricing. Easier still is proof in the form of a proclamation, where a public official commits a gaffe[195] by telling the truth. And when a German banker commits a gaffe, George Soros knows the truth: that the British pound will fall.

Fall it did, while an unnamed Bundesbank official said devaluation[196] of the pound was inevitable. Why? Because the Bank of England could not sustain a fixed exchange rate of 2.95 Deutschmark (DM) for each British pound (GBP).

In the end, Soros made $1 billion[197] by shorting the pound.

---

[195] Friedman, Nancy. "Word of the Week: Kinsley Gaffe." *Fritinancy*, 22 August 2011, https://nancyfriedman.typepad.com/away_with_words/2011/08/word-of-the-week-kinsley-gaffe.html

[196] Huhne, Christopher. "Schlesinger: a banker's guilt: The president of the Bundesbank has been woefully indiscreet. But the Chancellor, too, is a diminished figure, says Christopher Huhne." *Independent*, 1 October 1992, www.independent.co.uk/voices/schlesinger-a-banker-s-guilt-the-president-of-the-bundesbank-has-been-woefully-indiscreet-but-the-chancellor-too-is-a-diminished-figure-says-christopher-huhne-1554949.html

[197] Catão, Luis A. V. "What Are Real Exchange Rates?" *International Monetary Fund*, 31 May 2018, www.imf.org/external/Pubs/FT/fandd/basics/42-real-exchange-rates.htm

Lost in the process was the fact that words have consequences. That they have the power to clarify what numbers confirm—the power to upend markets and change the world.

Lost in the words about Black Wednesday, or Soros's trade on September 16, 1992, was the lesson of Black Monday and the stock market crash on October 19, 1987.

Because of what Treasury Secretary James A. Baker III[198] had said the Saturday before the crash, traders panicked. They panicked because he favored a fall in the dollar and did not seem to fear the fallout from a currency war. They panicked because he was no statesman as secretary of the treasury and no visionary in his subsequent role as secretary of state.

Two days later, the Dow Jones Industrial Average (DJIA) fell 508 points, or 22.6 percent. It was the largest one-day percentage drop[199] to date.

Perhaps Baker underestimated the currency of language and the power of words. Or perhaps he knew—quite well—that words are policies.

Either he dismissed the value of words, or he knew from experience, after managing two presidential campaigns and serving as White House chief of staff, that words have powerful consequences. Either he had no time for words, or he knew that words constitute a choice. He knew that silence before evil is evil while outrage against

---

[198] Redburn, Tom. "Germany Is Cautioned on Interest Rates: Baker Warns Further Hikes May Bring U.S. to Foster Fall in Dollar." *Los Angeles Times*, 18 October 1987, www.latimes.com/archives/la-xpm-1987-10-18-mn-15286-story.html

[199] "Worst days in the history of Dow Jones Industrial Average index 1897-2021." *Statista Research Department*, 25 February 2022, www.statista.com/statistics/261797/the-worst-days-of-the-dow-jones-index-since-1897/

evil is necessary, and that there is nothing evil about the necessity of opposing the focus of evil[200] in the modern world.

Words give us the power to fight evil.

As for the words of James Baker and his role as a policeman of White House traffic with control of all in and out paper flow to President Reagan, as well as his (Baker's) signature on all paper money during Reagan's second term: I believe the words undermine Baker's reputation as a successful power broker. As for his words on behalf of Reagan's successor, the record is a restatement of the obvious and a statement in defense of the odious.

The written record also fails to convey the frankness of Baker's oral communiques. The sound of his words weakens the soundness of his conclusions. That sound registers in a range of frequencies, and the words whistle with suggestive language.

The range includes nine words about the Balkans and a three-word comment starting with a four-letter word about the Jews.

The first comment[201] forgoes the dog whistle of American politics for direct reference to the dog of American foreign policy, with Baker saying, "We do not have a dog in this fight."

---

[200] Reagan Foundation. (2009, April 3). *"Evil Empire" Speech by President Reagan—Address to the National Association of Evangelicals* [Video]. YouTube. https://youtu.be/FcSm-KAEFFA

[201] Goldfarb, Michael. "Srebrenica, 20 Years Later." *Politico*, 8 July 2015, www.politico.com/magazine/story/2015/07/srebrenica-20-years-later-119845

The second comment[202], "Fuck the Jews," is a quote of many variations and no official sources.

Both speak to the reality of situations—foreign and domestic—without speaking to those who misconstrued Baker's words.

If Baker meant to say we should let sleeping dogs lie and not let slip the dogs of war, that America should not intervene in the Balkans, he was wrong. And if Baker meant to say Otto von Bismarck was right—that Americans are a happily placed people while the whole of the Balkans is not worth the bones of a single Pomeranian grenadier—he was still wrong.

We did not have to enter a civil war to enforce the laws of war and tell the president again what this[203] was all about. Nor did we have to let a war run its course.

Nothing Baker said about the Balkans was helpful, just as nothing he said about Israel[204] was conducive to peace or convincing to a majority of Jewish voters.

What he said to Congressman Mel Levine of the House Foreign Affairs Committee was helpful to no one save Bill Clinton, who won 78 percent[205] of the Jewish vote in the 1992 presidential election.

---

202 Tibon, Amir. "Did James Baker Really Say 'F*** the Jews'? New Book Clarifies U.S. Diplomat's Infamous Quote." *Haaretz*, 29 September 2020, www.haaretz.com/us-news/2020-09-29/ty-article/.premium/did-james-baker-really-say-f-the-jews-new-book-clarifies-infamous-quote/0000017f-e04d-d568-ad7f-f36f76840000

203 Silber, Laura and Allan Little. (1997). *Yugoslavia: Death of a Nation*. Penguin Books. www.penguinrandomhouse.com/books/329666/yugoslavia-by-laura-silber/

204 "U.S.-Soviet Relations." *C-SPAN*, 13 June 1990, www.c-span.org/video/?12698-1/us-soviet-relations

205 "Post Election Report—November, 1992." *Frederick T. Steeper Papers at the Gerald R. Ford Presidential Library*, November 1992, www.fordlibrarymuseum.gov/library/document/0432/043200000-001.pdf

Baker said, “Everybody over there (in Israel) should know that the telephone number (of the White House) is 1-202-456-1414. When you’re serious about peace, call us.”

Between Baker’s words and the president’s actions, the unintended consequence was congressional opposition to the White House and Republican opposition to a budget deal between the White House and a Democratic Congress. The deal ended the president’s pledge[206] not to raise taxes.

In the transition between his loss and the transfer of power, the president spoke at West Point[207]. He said, “Leadership requires formulating worthy goals, persuading others of their virtue, and contributing one’s share of the common effort and then some.”

Few goals are so virtuous as to be self-evident, requiring no words of explanation or inspiration.

Where value exists, the goal is to speak well enough to have people come together.

Where words devalue a goal requiring common effort, silence is a virtue.

Where words reveal the virtues of a goal, eloquence has uncommon value.

Leadership requires a virtuoso communicator.

---

[206] NBC News. (2018, December 4). *1988 Flashback: George H.W. Bush Says, ‘Read My Lips: No New Taxes’* [Video]. YouTube. https://youtu.be/AdVSqSNHhVo

[207] Bush, George H.W. “Address at West Point.” *Miller Center*, 5 January 1993, https://millercenter.org/the-presidency/presidential-speeches/january-5-1993-address-west-point

CHAPTER 7
The End of the Beginning

"This is the lesson that history teaches: repetition."
—Gertrude Stein

The lesson this book teaches is that it is better to study history than to repeat the crimes, follies, and misfortunes of mankind. In learning this, you will also come to see that it is better to know where and for what one should stand than to do nothing. And for this reason, I stand for clarity. I demand clarity—not because I have an aversion to risk, but because I demand to know what I risk losing.

My tolerance for risk varies depending on the nature of the investment. But I refuse to risk anything without knowing everything about an investment in advance, for all investing is a series of questions and answers. For every question, I want an answer. For every answer, I want proof. And for every unanswerable question, I want to know why there is no answer.

The overriding question is: What does an investment guarantee?

If an investment has no guarantee, tell me.

If a similar but less expensive investment exists, *tell me*.

If an investment guarantees a certain return, show it to me in writing.

About the costs, terms, and conditions of an investment, I should know everything.

And remember: Nothing is so new as to be extraordinary. This is especially true when viewing the past. Nothing is new from where I stand or what I have seen—and I saw two planes kill more people in one day than 348[208] German bombers did the first night of the Blitz.

I saw Cantor Fitzgerald lose more people than there were German bombers, with 658[209] employees killed on September 11, 2001, compared to 430[210] Londoners on September 7, 1940.

I saw two planes kill more people in one morning than 414 [211] Japanese planes had on the morning of December 7, 1941.

I saw planes crash into buildings until the buildings and the people inside them were no more.

I saw my brother carry the dead with him, on him, in a shroud of dust and debris.

I saw terror invade the streets of Manhattan and reality defeat the war on terror.

---

208 van der Drift, Nicky. "The Blitz." *International Bomber Command Centre*, 4 June 2020, https://internationalbcc.co.uk/about-ibcc/news/the-blitz/

209 THR Staff. "Out of the Clear Blue Sky: Film Review." *Hollywood Reporter*, 6 September 2013, www.hollywoodreporter.com/movies/movie-reviews/clear-blue-sky-film-review-623133/

210 "The Blitz Around Britain." *IWM*, www.iwm.org.uk/history/the-blitz-around-britain

211 "The Path to Pearl Harbor." *The National WWII Museum*, www.nationalww2museum.org/war/articles/path-pearl-harbor

I saw markets crash and businesses fail, and the rise of businesses too big to fail.

*

"Our world is increasingly complex, often chaotic, and always fast-flowing. This makes forecasting something between tremendously difficult and actually impossible, with a strong shift toward the latter as timescales get longer."

—Andrew McAfee, *Machine, Platform, Crowd: Harnessing Our Digital Future*

I see no reason to revise my words about the nature of man or the nature of certain man-made things.

Regarding financial markets, I see how easy it is to overlook the events preceding a major event. Especially when there is proof beyond a reasonable doubt that the probability of a crash is high. And when I look back on the bursting of the U.S. housing bubble and the onset of the Great Recession, I see the stubbornness of opinion versus the starkness of truth.

I saw then and see now how systems collapse. I saw that it pays to pay attention, because the ability to compare events starts with the willingness to observe events. If a prediction treats prices as massless quantities with limitless speed, and if all life exists within the weightless economy[212] of abstraction, then prices will fall and panic will ensue. But that fall does not have a fixed date.

This fact—that it is impossible to time markets with the regularity by which we predict the time and location of things in the

[212] "Economics A-Z terms beginning with A." *Economist*, www.economist.com/economics-a-to-z

physical universe—does not stop people from issuing financial predictions.

Consider the nature of financial predictions within the context of nature itself, because the difficulty of predicting one facet of nature—weather—is so hard as to humble the best meteorologists and mathematicians.

Consider that the supercomputers the U.S. government uses to track weather are among the fifty most powerful computers in the world.

Consider, too, that the government uses the world's fastest supercomputer[213] to simulate nuclear weapons explosions.

Now, if a supercomputer with the power to do 1.1 quintillion calculations per second can produce a five-day weather forecast with 90 percent[214] accuracy—and if that percentage applies to all places—are we to believe an investor can meet or exceed that performance with his own five-day forecast for all markets and individual stocks?

And if a ten-day weather forecast is no more accurate than a coin toss, are we to believe an investor can divine the future?

*

"Markets can influence the events that they anticipate."
—George Soros

When the probability of a major event increases during financial events, an investor waits. The same is true when all available

---

[213] Musil, Steven. "US Reclaims Supercomputing Crown With AMD-Powered Frontier." *CNET*, 30 March 2022, www.cnet.com/tech/computing/us-reclaims-supercomputing-crown-with-amd-powered-frontier/

[214] "How Reliable Are Weather Forecasts?" *SciJinks*, https://scijinks.gov/forecast-reliability/

evidence points to big profits from a big short or long position, or when the position is right but the arrival unknown.

This strategy is the investment strategy that Michael Lewis chronicles in *The Big Short*. In the book[215] and film[216] of the same name, we see how trust distorts reality. We see how trust corrupts intelligence when the people whose job it is to analyze and grade intelligence say the economy is sound and the housing market secure.

We see what happens when evidence trumps euphoria. We see the evidence in the sand states[217] of California, Florida, Nevada, and Arizona.

From California's Central Valley to the darkness of the Las Vegas Valley, among the sprawl of unfinished houses, empty buildings, and barren construction sites, we see the result of a big lie. And among the ghost towns, which look like doom towns[218] from a nuclear blast site, there lies debt.

The big lie Wall Street told investors about debt, that the securitization of bad debt was a good thing and that mortgage-backed securities were high-quality goods, made the lie credible. That lie made lies on paper creditable and commercial paper creditworthy, to the point where capitalism looked

---

215 Lewis, Michael. (2011). *The Big Short: Inside the Doomsday Machine*. W.W. Norton & Company. https://wwnorton.com/books/9780393338829

216 *The Big Short | Official Trailer*. Directed by Adam McKay, performances by Christian Bale, Steve Carell, Ryan Gosling, and Brad Pitt, Paramount Pictures, 2015. YouTube, uploaded by Paramount Movies, 16 March 2016 https://youtu.be/2v3PHtBVX4E

217 Olesiuk, Shayna M. and Kathy R. Kalser. "The Sand States: Anatomy of a Perfect Housing—Market Storm." *FDIC Quarterly*, vol. 3, no. 1, 2009, www.fdic.gov/analysis/quarterly-banking-profile/fdic-quarterly/2009-vol3-1/vol3-1-sand-states.pdf

218 "Intense Footage of Fake Towns Used for 1950s Nuclear Tests." *Smithsonian Magazine*, www.smithsonianmag.com/videos/intense-footage-of-fake-towns-used-for-1950s-n/

like socialism: a workers' paradise of McMansions, SUVs, and free money.

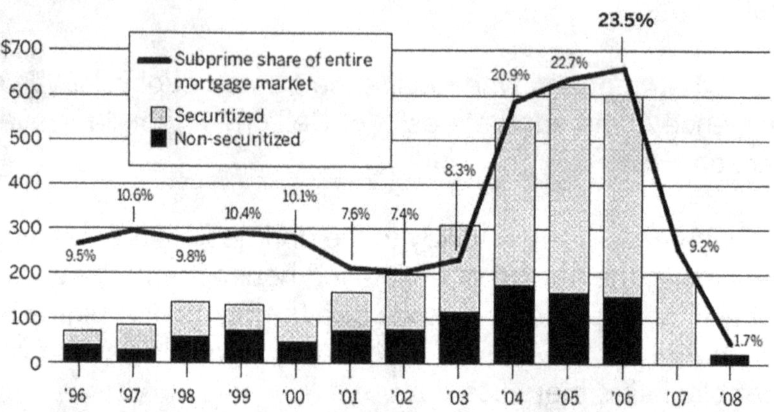

We should all live so well, in a world where every man is a king but no man wears a crown. Where we long not for the politics of a demagogue like Huey Long[219], but live according to the lyrics of his song, with castles and clothing and food for all.

Despite the dream of eternal sunshine and peace without end, we would be wise to remember the past. For it is the past that reminds us of false promises. It is the past that shows us politicians who speak like kings—including the Kingfish[220] himself—

[219] Long, Huey P. and Castro Carazo. "Every Man a King." *Tulane University Digital Library*, March 1935, https://digitallibrary.tulane.edu/islandora/object/tulane%3A19147

[220] "Huey Long." *Social Security History*, www.ssa.gov/history/hlong1.html

and those who promise[221] a chicken for every pot while ignoring the lessons of the past.

The promises of the past, with allowances for changes in technology and transportation, are not new.

The promise that there is to be no peasant so poor that he will not have a chicken in his pot every Sunday—a grandiose pledge by a grandiloquent king, still and contemplative in living art—remains elusive.

There are lessons, though.

First, there's the lesson that history has no shortage of broken promises. Second, we're taught that history is full of similar promises and outcomes, from the aftermath of a return to normalcy to the new normal of how we live now. Third, we can learn that excessive margin borrowing and excessive mortgage debt spread across markets.

The spread begins with a series of shifts and cracks, a sometimes slow but noticeable process of instability, where companies fail and industries falter. It may crash the stock market or destroy the housing market, resulting in a depression or the worst recession since the Great Depression.

If an investor knows where to look or what to look for, if he does as Lewis says all analysts should do and performs the nitty-gritty analysis, he can protect himself. And if he has a sense of history or an eye for history, he can read the signs—the signals, not the noise—that define history.

With that said, I offer the following as an example of what I mean.

---

221 "A Chicken for Every Pot" Political Ad. *State Historical Society of Iowa*, 30 October 1928, https://iowaculture.gov/history/education/educator-resources/primary-source-sets/great-depression-and-herbert-hoover/chicken

Disneyland *almost* never closes. The exceptions[222] are so rare as to be earth-shattering. The first exception was just that—earth-shattering: a 6.7-magnitude earthquake on January 17, 1994. The other two closings were a national day of mourning on November 23, 1963, the morning after the assassination of President Kennedy, and a morning[223] without an opening on the day of the September 11 attacks.

So when Shanghai Disneyland and Hong Kong Disneyland closed on January 25, 2020[224], and Tokyo Disneyland closed on February 29, 2020[225], and when the first of these things happened two months before shutdowns[226] began in America, I knew things were serious.

When Disney CEO Bob Iger first resigned on Friday, February 25, 2020[227], I knew things were bad indeed.

While I knew things would worsen, I did not know how long this time would last. I knew what to expect, despite not knowing how markets would react or individual stocks (including Disney) would

---

222 Lange, Jeva. "Disneyland has only closed unexpectedly 3 times. Now it's closing for the rest of the month." *The Week*, 13 March 2020, https://theweek.com/speedreads/901949/disneyland-only-closed-unexpectedly-3-times-now-closing-rest-month?amp

223 "Disneyland Was Closed on September 11, 2001." *Our Magical Disney Moments*, 11 September 2021, https://collinsrace1.wordpress.com/2021/09/11/disneyland-was-closed-on-september-11-2001/

224 Associated Press. "'A very special moment': Shanghai Disneyland reopens with precautions after coronavirus shutdown." *USA Today*, 11 May 2020, www.usatoday.com/story/travel/news/2020/05/11/coronavirus-shanghai-disneyland-becomes-first-disney-park-reopen/3107096001/

225 Reuters staff. "Tokyo Disneyland to stay closed through early April due to virus." *Reuters*, 10 March 2020, www.reuters.com/article/us-health-coronavirus-disneyland-idUSKBN20Y0KL

226 "COVID-19 Timeline." *David J. Sencer CDC Museum: In Association with the Smithsonian Institution*, www.cdc.gov/museum/timeline/covid19.html

227 Niu, Evan. "Was This the Real Reason Disney's Bob Iger Stepped Down Prematurely?" *The Motley Fool*, 21 March 2020, www.fool.com/investing/2020/03/21/was-this-the-real-reason-disneys-bob-iger-stepped.aspx

perform from one day to the next. And I knew to prepare rather than prophesize or panic. That mindset made all the difference.

When Iger returned on November 20, 2022[228], Disney's troubles were a matter of public record. His return does not, however, augur Disney's resurrection. (Not that Disney is dead or in terminal decline. Nor is the company in a state like Apple was prior to the return of Steve Jobs.)

Iger's return guarantees nothing, least of all a positive return on investment. Whether his return is his third and final act, thus following the three-act structure of a standard Disney film, is unclear. If his return is anticlimactic—if he does not fix Disney—the reason may be that Iger is in his third act while Disney's story is still in its second act.

If the stories do not converge, and Iger's journey does not resemble the hero's journey, this much is clear: life is not like a Disney story.

Not everyone gains a heart of wisdom or has a heart of compassion.

Not everyone lives a long life or rejoices in the beauty of life.

And no one gains the whole world and saves his soul.

*

"It is better to be roughly right than precisely wrong."
—John Maynard Keynes

Leave it to an economist with a degree in mathematics to speak to the contradictions of economics, saying (in effect)

---

[228] Calia, Mike and Alex Sherman. "Bob Iger returns as Disney CEO, replacing Bob Chapek after a brief, tumultuous tenure." *CNBC*, 20 November 2022, www.cnbc.com/2022/11/21/bob-iger-named-disney-ceo-effective-immediately.html

that mathematics is right because it is precise while the precision of an economic theory is only right if it works in the real world.

Leave it to Keynes[229] to question the science of a social science like economics, saying, "[T]oo large a proportion of recent 'mathematical' economics are mere concoctions, as imprecise as the initial assumptions they rest on, which allow the author to lose sight of the complexities and interdependencies of the real world in a maze of pretentious and unhelpful symbols."

Leave it to the economist Joan Robinson[230] to repeat the lesson that history teaches, that normality is a fiction of economic textbooks and there is no such thing as a normal period of history.

If normality is a state of equilibrium between man and nature—meaning man is an automaton within the self-operating machine of nature—no such thing exists. And if normality is the state of being usual, typical, or expected, no such state exists between man and his fellow man.

No such state exists between peoples either. The history of all hitherto existing tribes and nations is the history of struggles. Just look at the story of the first family—of paradise lost and the mark of the firstborn son—or even the nation's ongoing story of brother against brother.

If a state where the best conditions were prevalent existed, and peace and prosperity were dominant, normality would still be elusive. In this state, the splendid isolation of the past

---

[229] Keynes, John Maynard. (2016). *General Theory Of Employment, Interest And Money*. Atlantic Publishers & Dist. https://books.google.com/books/about/General_Theory_Of_Employment_Interest_An.html?id=xpw-96rynOcC

[230] [Excerpt]. In J. Robinson (1978). Contributions to Modern Economics (p. 3). Publisher. Retrieved from Google Books: https://www.google.com.ph/books/edition/Contributions_to_Modern_Economics/Py2jBQAAQBAJ?hl=en&gbpv=1&pg=PA3&printsec=frontcover

would recede into the past, compelling people to see things as they are. For there is a season and a time of change to everything, from the cycles of history to the history of the business cycle.

Capitalism requires the perennial gale of creative destruction[231]. So then, change is the engine of history and the impulse that keeps the capitalist engine in motion. The gale sweeps across the shore with a tattle-tale sound, slashing ships and sinking them in a freshwater storm of wind and fury. This storm creates waves greater than the swells across the Great Lakes, destroying companies without damaging the shoreline or flooding the buildings along Lake Shore Drive, because the gale of economics is a work of man and not nature.

The work in question is Joseph Schumpeter's *Capitalism, Socialism, and Democracy*[232]. In it, Schumpeter speaks of the wind and waves without referring to the sea. He makes his point by train instead of boat, which is to say he cites the railroad as an example of the power of creative destruction. His point applies to all industries, including the one-time retailer for the world, whose tower is still the tallest building in Chicago: Sears, Roebuck & Co. There, as in the pages of the Sears catalog, the gale of creative destruction endures.

The gale resounds with tales of woe and cries of sorrow. It is a warning from the dead, among whose ranks Sears is one of many, to the living. The gale tasks the living with the freedom to change or die, because no company is immune to change, and no investor is invulnerable to change.

*

---

231 . Schumpeter, Joseph A. (2003). *Capitalism, Socialism and Democracy*. Taylor & Francis e-Library. http://ia802305.us.archive.org/19/items/j.-schumpeter-capitalism-socialism-and-democracy/J.%20Schumpeter%20-%20Capitalism%2C%20Socialism%20and%20Democracy.pdf

232 Ibid

"Remembrance of things past is not necessarily the remembrance of things as they were."

—Marcel Proust, *In Search of Lost Time*

The past is as dynamic as the present and as distant as the future.

The past is a century-long story of a department store in a book, ending not only with the end of the Sears catalog but the end (in bankruptcy) of Sears itself.

Sears, a catalog of slogans—"a store with everything, by a store for everyone"—is no longer where America shops. And as a catalog of history—with its cover art[233] of the goddess Abundantia and her cornucopia, with the personification of prosperity standing as the colossus of the Chicago World's Fair—the Sears catalog reflects the exuberance of America.

The goddess also carries a letter in lieu of a staff, blazing a trail of clouds beneath which lay factories and farms. There, the ground overflows with goods, from bicycles and banjos to rifles and rocking chairs.

Here is the cover of America the Bountiful, her beauty bold and colorful like the lyrics of "America the Beautiful." Here is the American dream in a box, with a mortgage from Sears, a phonograph to play the song, and a home[234] in which to live the song.

Here, too, is home and auto insurance from Allstate[235], a division (until 1995) of Sears.

Here is the big book of retail, by a retailer with a former listing on the big board of the New York Stock Exchange.

---

[233] "1898-1930 Sears Catalog Covers." *Chicagology*, 17 March 2003, http://chicagology.com/sears/searscatalogs01/

[234] "Sears Homes 1908-1914." *Sears Archives*, www.searsarchives.com/homes/1908-1914.htm

[235] "Our History." *Allstate*, www.allstatecorporation.com/about/our-history.aspx

Here *was* (in 1964[236]) the publisher of a 626-page Christmas catalog—with 300 pages in full color—for eleven million families throughout America.

Here was a pre-digital everything store selling socks and stocks[237] under one roof.

Here lies a graveyard of few grave markers, where the survivors number twenty stores across a dozen states and no survivors remain in the Prairie State. Here, the state of the Sears complex[238] in the North Lawndale area of Chicago is dead.

The grounds of this second city are more vacant than vibrant. The Printing Building has no pressroom and the Advertising Building no saleroom, for both buildings no longer exist.

Most of the campus buildings no longer exist, making it seem as if the Power House were a kiln of destruction in which red bricks burn as firebricks and the smokestack scatters the ashes of the dead.

Southwest of the remains of this city lies the town of Cicero, Illinois, where the light of the Western Electric Company no longer shines and the Hawthorne Works[239] no longer stands. The remains give new meaning to the words of the town's namesake, that "History is the witness of the times, the light of truth, the life of memory, the teacher of life, the messenger of antiquity."

---

236 "Sears Catalogue Issued." *New York Times*, 25 September 1964, www.nytimes.com/1964/09/25/archives/sears-catalogue-issued.html

237 Hagerty, James R. "Robert Gardiner, Wall Street Giant, Helped Sears With 'Socks and Stocks' Strategy." *The Wall Street Journal*, 16 November 2018, www.wsj.com/articles/robert-gardiner-wall-street-giant-helped-sears-with-socks-and-stocks-strategy-1542382920

238 Stevens, Caroline Nye. "The Sears, Roebuck and Co. Complex, North Lawndale." *Blueprint: Chicago*, 23 April 2012, http://www.blueprintchicago.org/2012/04/23/the-sears-roebuck-co-complex-north-lawndale/

239 "Western Electric Hawthorne Plant." *Chicagology*, http://chicagology.com/skyscrapers/skyscrapers116/

The remains bear silent witness to the destruction of physical evidence.

But for the original Sears Tower[240] and the Works' water tower[241]—the two visible to each other across a plain of Prairie-style houses and brick bungalows—nothing remains of either complex. And because of the long, low landscape between the two, no works speak to the history of the Works as the nation's largest telephone factory.

[240] Coleman, Katie. "Former Sears Complex Returns as a Beacon in a Chicago Neighborhood." *New York Times*, 12 March 2019, www.nytimes.com/2019/03/12/business/sears-chicago-homan-square.html?smid=nytcore-ios-share&referringSource=articleShare

[241] Hawthorne Works Tower Photo: Hawthorne Works tower 2012 1 [Photograph]. Retrieved from Wikimedia Commons: https://en.wikipedia.org/wiki/Hawthorne_Works#/media/File%3AHawthorne_Works_tower_2012_1.JPG

There is a complex history behind this castle of a complex and its seven-story tower at the corner of 22nd Street and Cicero Avenue. From this tower, where no walls enclose the grounds and no gates open onto the grounds, history marches in silence. This silence is both ironic and sad.

The procession passes shadows cast by memories of a sprawling complex, of running tracks and railroad tracks, where workers play and factories pay workers a living wage.

History notes the missing, where the grounds bear no signs of the fire department, hospital, park, social center, tennis courts, gymnasium, and retail store. These grounds contain the lesson that history teaches about industry and power: that creative destruction can raze buildings and breach walls without the sound of trumpets or the beating of drums.

Lost in the destruction is the enormity of the past. Most people now live with no working memory of Sears or Western Electric, and with no knowledge of the lives of the workers of Chicagoland.

The lesson for investors is that the title of personhood does not entitle a business to live forever. Today's leader may be tomorrow's laggard, and what ails one may annihilate all.

Industries rise and fall, just as some companies create change or succumb to it.

What does not change is the lesson that history teaches: that history is an argument without end.

Here again, irony abounds. Because those who study the past must contend with those who focus on the future, history has no shortage of futurists and no surplus of accurate predictions of the future from the past.

The rebuttal to the false optimism of the futurist is the reality of the present. Articles from the past read like pieces from an alternate reality, and articles in *Bloomberg*[242] and *Harvard Business Review*[243] (*HBR*) read like advertorials for Sears.

Bloomberg takes a less promotional stance than *HBR*, as the latter resets the story and offers a narrative fallacy about the transformation of Sears. Both outlets repeat the story about the return of Sears without mentioning the rise of Amazon. But *HBR* legitimizes the story, despite the authors' relationship with Sears. The result is a long and self-serving article in which the structure of the story justifies the use of structural equation modeling, such that the pieces—the arrows, ovals, rectangles, triangles, and squares—fit the title of the article: "The Employee-Customer-Profit Chain at Sears."

The article leaves no room for the demise of Sears or the death of department stores. Missing, too, are the words internet, e-commerce, and online sales. Some of the words appear in the company's annual report[244], where the then-chairman and CEO lists the five key priorities for 1999.

The fourth priority lists electronic commerce last, after home services and direct response, as a way to accelerate new growth. The fifth priority, "to aggressively manage costs and cash flow," softens "the softer side of Sears"[245] into a purée for the toothless and the timid. It is a themeless pudding that no executive should serve and no shareholder should accept.

---

242 Weimer, De'Ann. "The Softest Side Of Sears." *Bloomberg*, 27 December 1998, www.bloomberg.com/news/articles/1998-12-27/the-softest-side-of-sears

243 Rucci et al. "The Employee-Customer-Profit Chain at Sears." *Harvard Business Review*, January–February 1998, https://hbr.org/1998/01/the-employee-customer-profit-chain-at-sears

244 Sears. (1998). *Annual report*. Retrieved from www.searsarchives.com/history/annual_reports/1998/cl.htm

245 Martinez, Arthur C. and Charles Madigan. (2001). *The Hard Road to the Softer Side: Lessons from the Transformation of Sears*. Crown Business. https://books.google.com/books?id=cjIPAQAAMAAJ&focus=searchwithinvolume&q=softer+side

The takeaway of this story is an order—to take away the extraneous, the ambiguous, the unclear; to never give in to feelings of unreasoning fancy or unwarranted folly.

*

"Surely the apple is the noblest of fruits. Let the most beautiful or the swiftest have it. That should be the 'going' price of apples."

—Henry David Thoreau

The going price for a share of Apple stock was 78 cents (split-adjusted), when Michael Dell[246] recommended shutting the company down and giving the money back to the shareholders.

No doubt Dell thought Apple was dead, regardless of Steve Jobs's return to Apple or Jobs's plan to revive Apple. He thought he was right, regardless of what Jobs said or did. He thought Jobs was wrong, regardless of Jobs's thoughts on Apple.

ut it was Dell who was wrong. Not because he was too nearsighted to see the future, but because he was too narrow-minded to connect the facts at the time.

While he could not have foreseen a march of rapid progress and record profits, or a revolution in retail and the release of a series of revolutionary devices, he could have inferred that neither Apple nor Microsoft believed he was right.

Dell issued his recommendation two months after Microsoft invested $150 million[247] in Apple and less than a month after Jobs unveiled

---

[246] Singh, Jai. "Dell: Apple should close shop." *CNET*, 6 October 1997, www.cnet.com/tech/tech-industry/dell-apple-should-close-shop/

[247] Kawamoto, Dawn. "Microsoft to invest $150 million in Apple." *CNET*, 6 January 2009, www.cnet.com/tech/tech-industry/microsoft-to-invest-150-million-in-apple/

his vision[248] for Apple. He ignored the fact that the investment was a pecuniary check against charges of predatory pricing. And he did not see how the case for one weakened the antitrust case against the other, or that what was good for Apple was not bad for Microsoft.

Had he seen things differently—or seen the strategy behind Apple's "Think Different"[249] advertising campaign—perhaps he would have seen that Apple was a lifestyle brand.

Perhaps he would have seen how the brand's (mostly post-humous) ambassadors transcended technology. Perhaps he would've noticed how Apple married technology with liberal arts and the humanities through the likes of Einstein, Earhart, and Edison.

Perhaps he would have also seen how Apple transcended time, joining together *Time*'s "Man of the Year" from 1930 (Mahatma Gandhi) with their 1963 honoree (Martin Luther King Jr.), among others, in a one-minute act of wish fulfillment.

The campaign married words with deeds, culminating in Apple's last event at the Flint Center in Cupertino, California, and the first of several new product launches by Jobs on behalf of Apple. This event marked a change in design, starting with the introduction of the iMac[250] in Bondi Blue, whose translucent case and not-so-mighty mouse Jobs called "gorgeous."

Jobs also changed the discourse surrounding Apple. He compared the company to global powerhouses Nike, Disney, and Sony. (Not for nothing did Jobs become Disney's larg-

---

248 Rene Brokop. (2013, April 21). *Best marketing strategy ever! Steve Jobs Think different / Crazy ones speech* [Video]. YouTube. https://youtu.be/keCwRdbwNQY

249 vintagemacmuseum. (2010, May 23). *Apple—Here's to the Crazy Ones (1997)* [Video]. YouTube. https://youtu.be/tjgtLSHhTPg

250 "Apple unveils iMac." *CNNfn*, 6 May 1998, https://money.cnn.com/1998/05/06/technology/apple/

est shareholder in 2006, after Disney bought Pixar[251] for $7.4 billion.)

Jobs lyricized the lesson that history teaches, with the help of the ad agency TBWA Chiat/Day, whose words[252] he recorded and whose work complemented Apple's best work.

Jobs repeated his intentions for Apple, based on his regrets about Apple, saying, "[T]here have been moments when we haven't been proud of Apple."

He closed by saying Apple was on the rebound.

After the close of the stock market on Friday, January 13, 2006, he sent an email[253] to Apple employees, which read:

Team, it turned out that Michael Dell wasn't perfect at predicting the future. Based on today's stock market close, Apple is worth more than Dell. Stocks go up and down, and things may be different tomorrow, but I thought it was worth a moment of reflection today. Steve.

The message repeats the lesson that experience teaches: that life is unpredictable.

---

[251] La Monica, Paul R. "Disney buys Pixar. House of Mouse is teaming up with Pixar in a $7.4 billion deal. Steve Jobs to become board member at Disney." *CNNMoney.com*, 25 January 2006, https://money.cnn.com/2006/01/24/news/companies/disney_pixar_deal/

[252] ChronoDesign. (2011, October 25). *The Crazy Ones—Steve Jobs narrated ver.—Think Different* [Video]. YouTube. https://youtu.be/uKUMJdTJiX8

[253] Markoff, John. "Michael Dell Should Eat His Words, Apple Chief Suggests." *New York Times*, 16 January 2006, www.nytimes.com/2006/01/16/technology/michael-dell-should-eat-his-words-apple-chief-suggests.html?smid=nytcore-ios-share&referringSource=articleShare

Looking back on Steve Jobs's life, his message reflects an aesthetic that determines aesthetics: a two-in-one style of dress and design in which function follows form.

The message reflects a passion for greatness and the presentation of "insanely great"[254] products in which the personal is professional—or in which I, the singular, first-person pronoun, is "i," as in the iMac, the iPod, the iPhone, and the iPad.

The "i"[255] stands for many things, according to Jobs: internet, individual, instruct, inform, and inspire. And the "i" excludes Michael Dell's recommendation to investors, because the lesson that he teaches is that predictions are unreliable.

The lesson that readers should repeat to themselves is that evidence matters.

We have more lessons to learn.

---

[254] Kawasaki, Guy. "Guy Kawasaki: At Apple, Steve Jobs divided people into 2 groups—'insanely great' and 'crappy.'" *CNBC*, 9 April 2019, www.cnbc.com/amp/2019/04/05/apple-steve-jobs-divided-people-into-2-groups-insanely-great-and-crappy-people-says-ex-employee-guy-kawasaki.html

[255] JoshuaG. (2006, January 30). *The First iMac Introduction* [Video]. YouTube. https://youtu.be/0BHPtoTctDY

CHAPTER 8

The Financial Translator

> ***"It is the task of the translator to release in his own language that pure language that is under the spell of another, to liberate the language imprisoned in a work in his re-creation of that work."***
>
> —Walter Benjamin,
> *Illuminations: Essays and Reflections*

All life is a work of translation, from the beginning of the first traces of life on Earth to the Word in the beginning.

All history is a study of translation, too—from the words of the Father of History to the *Lives*[256] of "a bible for heroes;" from the heroes of Julius Caesar's *Civil Wars* to his own heroism in the Gallic Wars; from the Nazarene's words in the Bible to his saying unto them, "Render to Caesar the things that are Caesar's, and to G-d the things that are G-d's."

All money is also a form of translation, from the inscription on a Roman coin to the words on all U.S. paper money and coins. And those words say, "In G-d We Trust."

---

[256] Emerson, Ralph Waldo. (1904). *The Complete Works*. Bartleby.com. www.bartleby.com/90/1011.html

Even if we were all believers of the same faith and readers of the same Bible, with firmness in the rightness of G-d, we could not return to the beginning of one language and one speech. Even if we were all believers in the G-d of the universe and speakers of the language G-d talks, which is to say even if we were all numerate in the extreme and literate in calculus, we would still need translators.

Speech is the currency of existence and language is the dollar of diplomacy. The wrong word can invite war and the right man can use words to war against evil. And so, every word counts.

Numbers also count, given one man's account of service for his country. Such is the case of *Thirteen Days*[257], Robert F. Kennedy's memoir of the Cuban Missile Crisis. The book is a testament to the power of words and the presentation of evidence, culminating in an exchange of letters and peace without war.

Some of the words[258] do not require translation, when, for example, Adlai Stevenson, then U.S. ambassador to the United Nations, says, "Do you, Ambassador [Valerian] Zorin, deny that the U.S.S.R. has placed and is placing medium- and intermediate-range missiles and sites in Cuba? Yes or no—don't wait for the translation—yes or no?"

But for this display before the public, credit belongs to the private correspondence[259] between President Kennedy and Soviet leader

---

[257] Kennedy, Robert F. (1999). *Thirteen Days: A Memoir of the Cuban Missile Crisis*. W.W. Norton & Company. https://wwnorton.com/books/Thirteen-Days/

[258] Lindsay, James M. "TWE Remembers: Adlai Stevenson Dresses Down the Soviet Ambassador to the UN (Cuban Missile Crisis, Day Ten)." *Council on Foreign Relations*, 25 October 2012, www.cfr.org/blog/twe-remembers-adlai-stevenson-dresses-down-soviet-ambassador-un-cuban-missile-crisis-day-ten

[259] Blight, James G. (2012). *The Armageddon Letters: Kennedy, Khrushchev, Castro in the Cuban Missile Crisis*. Rowman & Littlefield. https://rowman.com/ISBN/9781442216815/The-Armageddon-Letters-Kennedy-Khrushchev-Castro-in-the-Cuban-Missile-Crisis

Nikita Khrushchev. And because of the care responsible for the writing and translation of these letters, the world remembers what President Kennedy said eight months after this crisis, during his June 10, 1963, commencement address[260] at American University.

He said enmities between nations, as between individuals, do not last forever.

He also spoke to a nation half slave and half free, when, on June 26, 1963[261], he said, "All free men, wherever they may live, are citizens of Berlin, and, therefore, as a free man, I take pride in the words 'Ich bin ein Berliner.'"

Because we are all translators, I take pride in my role as a financial translator. I read to interpret, so I may convey what I translate. My job is to find the spirit in the letter of a text, so the message is direct and the investment opportunity understandable.

Where a literary translator works with an editor, I work with lawyers, entrepreneurs, and insurance professionals. My job is to verify what a text says and substantiate what I say regarding an investment opportunity. This way, the context is evident and the evidence clear.

*

"I know numbers are beautiful. If they aren't beautiful, nothing is."

—Paul Erdős

---

260 Kennedy, John F. "Commencement Address at American University." *John F. Kennedy Presidential Library and Museum*, 10 June 1963, www.jfklibrary.org/archives/other-resources/john-f-kennedy-speeches/american-university-19630610

261 Kennedy, John F. "Remarks in the Rudolph Wilde Platz." *John F. Kennedy Presidential Library and Museum*, 26 June 1963, www.jfklibrary.org/asset-viewer/archives/JFKWHA/1963/JFKWHA-200-001/JFKWHA-200-001

The number is a palindrome, or three ones—three odd integers—for which the sum is three.

The cardinal numeral is three words, or one hundred eleven.

The natural number is 111.

The number is also the age of a precedent, written by the namesake of a poet and a man of letters in his own right.

The precedent, Grigsby v. Russell[262], is (at the time of writing) 111-years-old.

In *Grigsby*, the U.S. Supreme Court designated life insurance policies as private property.

Writing for the majority of the Court, Justice Oliver Wendell Holmes said, "Life insurance has become in our days one of the best recognized forms of investment and self-compelled saving. So far as reasonable safety permits, it is desirable to give life policies the ordinary characteristics of property."

Life insurance is collateral, life insurance is security, life insurance is a wealth-building opportunity. Life insurance is a lifeline for the retiree of few means, the person or family of some means, and the investor of substantial means. Life insurance meets the financial test of self-government, regarding the young, the elderly, and the needy.

As for the moral test of government, the public life of Hubert H. Humphrey[263] represents the highest standard.

---

[262] *Grigsby v. Russell*, 222 U.S. 149 (1911). https://casetext.com/case/grigsby-v-russell

[263] Humphrey, Hubert H. "Address to the Democratic National Convention." *Minnesota Historical Society*, 13 July 1976, http://www2.mnhs.org/library/findaids/00442/pdfa/00442-04021.pdf

As for the rest of us—life insurance is a way to build a legacy and earn tax-free income.

*

"Ethics is knowing the difference between what you have a right to do and what is right to do."

—Potter Stewart

The teaching of business ethics is like the study of legal ethics. It is a rite of initiation rather than proof of an initiate's ability to do right and fight wrongdoing.

The teaching confirms the need for remedial instruction, for which adults pay to receive instruction, and by which other adults—professors—provide instruction. The teaching does not produce ethical bankers or exemplary lawyers. Rather, it reveals the existence of a moral deficit throughout society.

The fact that I must state this fact—that we have corrupt lawmakers and a general surplus of lawbreakers—reveals the severity of the deficit we face.

We have insider traders[264] in Congress and moral traitors[265] in business, making it hard for the ethical and good to do business.

---

[264] Levinthal, Dave and Madison Hall. "78 members of Congress have violated a law designed to prevent insider trading and stop conflicts-of-interest." *Business Insider*, 3 January 2023, www.businessinsider.com/congress-stock-act-violations-senate-house-trading-2021-9

[265] Pliner, Eric. "Welcome to the new ethical context." *Fortune*, 8 April 2022, https://fortune.com/2022/04/08/welcome-new-ethical-context-cancel-culture-corporate-scandals-dismissals-careers-executives-leadership-esg-dei-eric-pliner/

I write these words from experience, having witnessed lapses in judgment on Wall Street. I'm also a person with strong opinions about charges of lapsation[266] within the insurance industry.

Lapsation involves allegations of unlawful conduct regarding how an insurer allows its life insurance policies to lapse for nonpayment of a premium. Now, let me be clear about where I stand on this issue: I am an advocate of life insurance—but not an advocate for *any one* insurer. I am an insurance broker, not a captive insurance agent, which means I have no information to omit for the sake of a commission.

A captive agent is just that, a captive—a bondman—who is duty-bound to sell what his employer offers. A captive agent must do as his employer says and not as his client necessarily wishes.

The client is not in good hands, in my opinion, because the captive agent does not have the power to strengthen and give wealth to all. The captive agent does not have a free hand to deliver a client to the best of all available life insurance policies. In short, a captive agent does not have the freedom to do what is always best for a client.

In contrast to the agent who suppresses his conscience to satiate his captor, who obeys the law but violates the higher law, or who loses his vigilance and lets a life insurance policy lapse, I value virtue most.

I value freedom over fees. And I insist on oversight because I do not trust what I cannot prove.

*

[266] Miller et al. "What's Happening in California After McHugh?" *JD Supra*, 8 April 2022, www.jdsupra.com/legalnews/what-s-happening-in-california-after-9703274/

"If something cannot go on forever, it will stop."
—Herbert Stein, *What I Think: Essays on Economics, Politics, & Life*

So reads "Stein's Law," whose namesake was an adviser to presidents and the father of a speechwriter, Ben Stein[267], to a succession of presidents.

So reads a law of economic motion, in contrast to belief in the end of laws governing distance, speed, and direction.

To those who believe that financial markets always rise, Stein's Law counters exuberance with the hard evidence of reality. And to those who believe in the 60/40 portfolio rule[268], Stein's Law questions whether the rule is still valid.

When this rule has the worst return in 100 years—and when the rule of an average annual return of 9 percent produces a year-to-date loss of 34.4 percent[269]—a wise investor reviews his portfolio. Any investor who allocates 60 percent to stocks and 40 percent to bonds should reconsider the structure of his portfolio.

Sam Stovall, chief investment strategist at CFRA Research[270], says, "The market right now is going through a crisis of confidence." So, what insurers must do is save the many, so people may protect their savings.

---

[267] Stein, Ben. "Ben Stein's Diary." *The American Spectator*, https://spectator.org/author/bstein/

[268] Solberg, Lauren. "Why Your 60/40 Balanced Portfolio Isn't Working in 2022." *Morningstar.com*, 14 July 2022, www.morningstar.com/articles/1102108/why-your-6040-balanced-portfolio-isnt-working-in-2022

[269] Karaahmetovic, Senad. "Annualized Return on '60/40' Portfolio is -34.4%, Worst in Past 100 Years—BofA." *Investing.com*, 14 October 2022, www.investing.com/news/stock-market-news/annualized-return-on-6040-portfolio-is-344-worst-in-past-100-years--bofa-432SI-2912509

[270] Website: CFR Research. Retrieved from https://www.cfraresearch.com

Failure to act will result in a stoppage of incalculable stress and immeasurable loss. Tomorrow's retirees will have no way to live save expiring en masse, save death in lieu of destitution.

Without life insurance, those who need a safe and tax-free source of retirement income will not have one. And those unable to work will be unable to live.

Avoiding this scenario starts with alerting the public to the imminence of this threat. The writing and delivery of such a message is a charge the financial translator must assume and a role he must accept. The costs are minimal in comparison to the consequences of inaction.

To sound the alarm is to admonish the public, telling the many what to do and where to go.

To sound the alarm is not to sound like an alarmist, because the crisis we face is too extreme to exaggerate. If the crisis is hard to imagine, the financial translator must make it easy to understand.

If the crisis is hard to define, the financial translator must make it easy to describe. If the crisis is hard to stop, the insurance industry must make it easier to withstand.

The insurance industry must lead us through this crisis. This duty insures lives, providing for the defense of liberty and the pursuit of happiness. This duty demands exemplary counsel, by people of excellent character, for people in exigent circumstances. This duty belongs to the insurance industry, allowing it to earn what no amount of advertising can buy: the truth.

Honoring the truth enriches the lives of millions, exceeding the combined wealth of a thousand billionaires, because safety is a treasure of inestimable worth.

*

"Hypocrisy is a tribute that vice pays to virtue."
—François de La Rochefoucauld, *Reflections or Sentences and Moral Maxims*

I once told the patriarch of one of America's richest families how life insurance could help him. I told this man, whose wealth is in property, about the tax-saving properties of private placement life insurance (PPLI). And he listened.

When he asked me to speak to the Wall Street firm that manages his money, his advisers told him not to listen to me. When the firm released a product similar to my presentation, the patriarch listened to me instead.

The firm acted according to type—not because I was wrong, but because the people I had spoken to feared I was right. The firm put its interests ahead of the client's interests for fear of losing the client's business and not having a comparable product with which to conduct business.

Because the firm limited what it could do and how far it could go, the firm minded who got the credit—and the commissions—for any amount of good an outsider did for a client.

Thus did an adage about the greatest good, with pride of place in the Reagan White House[271], have no place on Wall Street.

[271] Reagan, Ronald. "Remarks at a Meeting of the White House Conference for a Drug Free America." *Ronald Reagan Presidential Foundation & Institute*, 29 February 1988, www.reaganfoundation.org/ronald-reagan/reagan-quotes-speeches/remarks-at-a-meeting-of-the-white-house-conference-for-a-drug-free-america/

The competition to get business, the competition to keep business, the competition to outcompete the competition—such is the nature of competition. The competition can be particularly unfair to the consumer, who pays for protection he does not need or overpays for protection that does not meet all his needs.

According to the 2022 Insurance Barometer Study[272], more than half the population thinks term life insurance is three times more expensive than it is. This study tells me the barometer is low, that a storm of doubt surrounds what people think about life insurance. This storm starts in the insurance industry, gathering strength as it spreads across incomes and communities.

About the message pertaining to the storm—that the storm threatens to foreclose opportunity and increase foreclosures, that we face losses due to words lost in translation and a breakdown in communication—the study underscores what I have said for years: that we must do better.

If we know the message is wrong and the danger is real, and if we retreat from reality and lose our will, the storm will worsen year by year until the reckoning comes. My duty is to correct the record and complete the message. Only then can we advance a cause worthy of Lincoln and be true to the words of the only president[273] born in the Land of Lincoln, for the words say, "We will always remember. We will always be proud. We will always be prepared, so we may always be free."

---

[272] Scalon et al. "2022 Insurance Barometer Study." *Equitable.com*, https://portal.equitable.com/appentry/EDoxRedirect?node_id=A2020082700016

[273] Reagan, Ronald. "Remarks at a United States-France Ceremony Commemorating the 40th Anniversary of the Normandy Invasion, D-day." *Ronald Reagan Presidential Library & Museum*, 6 June 1984, www.reaganlibrary.gov/archives/speech/remarks-united-states-france-ceremony-commemorating-40th-anniversary-normandy

Financial freedom is the work of the translator. It is the impact I work to achieve, and it is the work every person has a right to pursue or attain.

What follows is a declaration of rights and a statement of principles. It is a translation of the qualities that life insurance possesses and the means by which life insurance can improve a person's quality of life.

These qualities may be new to many. No doubt they are *news* to many life insurance agents, in whom clients stake their trust. But the qualities are real just the same.

The qualities that define life insurance, which I enumerate and explain in the chapters in this next section of the book, do not require trust. Because I trust what I can prove, I translate what I read with care for the reader. I also have no care for greetings in the marketplaces, or patience for pretense, as this book is my own reward. May this book have an impact on the teaching of investing.

CHAPTER 9

Sailing Home

"I pass with relief from the tossing sea of Cause and Theory to the firm ground of Result and Fact."

—Winston Churchill,
The Story of the Malakand Field Force

The firm ground is where the wise stand, safe from pinnacles that dissolve in the precipice.

About the sea below, red with debt and white with foam, and about the flotsam from those houses underwater and too deep to raise, here is a reminder: We must sail to port, for we cannot afford to drift or drop anchor. We must sail toward safety, in safety, with the safety life insurance provides. We must sail with the tide, allowing it to lift us without having it crash against us. And if we sail this path of safety, we may convert a rise in valuations into a plan that delivers everlasting value.

By using life insurance to create an estate plan, and by funding the plan with cash from a home equity conversion mortgage

(HECM[274]), qualified borrowers (ages sixty-two and older) can turn rising house prices into tax-free income.

Since the appraised value of a house determines the size of a loan, and since the inventory[275] of single-family homes is at a forty-year low, borrowers may have more money to invest.

How borrowers choose to invest this money—whether they choose to guarantee a legacy for their loved ones or better themselves without relying on their loved ones—is their choice. More important is that borrowers are free to choose. They have the freedom to secure paper wealth with paper as secure as property.

Because the law[276] says that life insurance is a form of property, and because life insurance offers liquidity, borrowers are free to make real the promises of HECM. They may bestow upon themselves, or bequeath to posterity, the blessings of financial freedom.

Take, for instance, a sixty-two-year-old woman with an average life expectancy of eighty-four.

According to the Government Accountability Office (GAO[277]), this woman is like 85 percent of Americans her age and older, in that she owns her own home. But she is also like most Americans over fifty-five in that she has no retirement savings. If she wants to retire at sixty-two—the earliest she can claim Social Security—

---

274 "Home Equity Conversion Mortgages for Seniors." *U.S. Department of Housing and Urban Development*, www.hud.gov/program_offices/housing/sfh/hecm/hecmhome

275 Alloway, Tracy and Joe Weisenthal. "Here's How Weird Things Are Getting in the Housing Market." *Bloomberg*, 10 October 2022, www.bloomberg.com/news/articles/2022-10-10/here-s-how-weird-things-are-getting-in-the-housing-market

276 *Grigsby v. Russell*, 222 U.S. 149 (1911). https://supreme.justia.com/cases/federal/us/222/149/

277 "Retirement Security: Most Households Approaching Retirement Have Low Savings." *GAO.gov*, 12 May 2015, www.gao.gov/products/gao-15-419

she needs to compensate for an additional five years without income.

So, she must either put her wants aside and work, or she must find a solution that works to her advantage.

If the appraised value of her home is $440,300[278]—the median sales price for houses sold in the United States—she can transfer the money from a HECM loan into a life insurance policy. In doing so, she safeguards the principal while earning tax-free income from a diversified portfolio of investments.

The beneficiaries of her estate can also receive a cash payout, minus the balance and interest of the HECM loan, thanks to a life insurance policy. The borrower requirements[279] say she must:

- Own the property outright or have paid down a considerable amount
- Occupy the property as her principal residence
- Not be delinquent on any federal debt
- Have financial resources to continue to make timely payment of ongoing property charges (such as property taxes, insurance, and Homeowner Association fees, etc.)
- Participate in a consumer information session given by a HUD-approved HECM counselor

Because life insurance is a lifeline, this woman has the power to avoid the shallows and miseries of the sea. Whether her voyage is long or short, whether her vessel is a sloop or a schooner, the sea—mysterious, wild, and unrestrained—endures.

---

[278] U.S. Census Bureau and U.S. Department of Housing and Urban Development, Median Sales Price of Houses Sold for the United States [MSPUS], retrieved from FRED, Federal Reserve Bank of St. Louis; https://fred.stlouisfed.org/series/MSPUS, January 16, 2023.

[279] "How the HECM Program Works." *U.S. Department of Housing and Urban Development*, www.hud.gov/program_offices/housing/sfh/hecm/hecmabou

To weather its storms and withstand its moods, to be like a rock of strength and prudence, requires the assurance of a wise captain.

The captain deserves insurance, too, so she may sail in peace, despite the conditions of the sea. Mindful of the direction and peaceful because of her directives, life insurance guides this captain home.

*

"The personal right to acquire property, which is a natural right, gives to property when acquired a right to protection as a social right."

—James Madison

From a downpour of tears to a deluge of debt, the loss of a loved one can drown a family in a sea of emotions and a storm of expenses.

The loss can flood the last refuge of sanctity and shelter, leaving a house underwater and a family homeless. It can leave a widow without a lifeline, a widower without a path to safety, and children without the means to pursue any number of life opportunities.

Consider the following:

- ➢ The number of foreclosure starts is up 219 percent[280] since the start of 2022, according to ATTOM Data Solutions.
- ➢ The number of foreclosure filings, including foreclosure starts, is up 153 percent from the same time a year ago.
- ➢ The number of properties with foreclosure filings is 164,581, or one in every 1,517 properties.

---

280 ATTOM Team, "Increased Foreclosure Activity in First Six Months of 2022 Approaches Pre-Covid Levels." *ATTOM*, 14 July 2022, www.attomdata.com/news/market-trends/foreclosures/attom-midyear-2022-u-s-foreclosure-market-report/

The number of properties repossessed through foreclosure is 10,515, up 39 percent from a year ago.

States with the highest foreclosure rates in 2022 were:

- Illinois (one in every 1,926 housing units)
- Delaware (one in every 2,387 housing units)
- South Carolina (one in every 2,417 housing units)
- New Jersey (one in every 2,441 housing units)
- Florida (one in every 2,950 housing units)

Given these dangers and the specific danger of losing a house to foreclosure, life insurance has the power to protect spouses and families from further suffering. And life insurance with mortgage protection allows families to shelter at home—to *stay in their homes*—rather than sheltering in place.

Rather than seeking temporary shelter or evacuating to emergency shelters, life insurance with mortgage protection not only diverts the course of a storm but dissipates it altogether. But families must first buy this protection, meaning insurers must explain why families—particularly young families—need life insurance with mortgage protection.

The explanation is a matter of basic math, where loss of life equals loss of income. This loss expands as bills accumulate and interest accrues, turning survivors of the hardest loss into nomads in a permanent state of hardship. Without life insurance, the worst hard times become hard times without end.

This scenario is no exaggeration, as too many live to survive while too few have the protection to live well. Avoiding this scenario requires the insurance industry to speak to the urgency of the issue. Emphasizing this issue—repeating the emphasis on having life insurance with mortgage protection—is a duty the insurance industry must honor.

Anything less is a disservice to those who need to know the truth: that this protection is indispensable to honoring the terms of a mortgage without mortgaging the strength or savings of the good. The good include families in pain, whose sorrow insurers can assuage through life insurance policies that are palliatives of a financial sort.

There palliatives may be curatives. These treatments may have restorative properties. And among these properties are the protection of property and a source of monthly income. In the end, all these goods are just and righteous.

However, insurers must promote this message. And if they think people view themselves as prospects and that consumers treat themselves as contacts, then they need to rethink everything. The same is true if insurers think lack of contact corresponds to lack of interest, or if they think consumers have no interest in life insurance with mortgage protection.

The insurance industry has a chance to broadcast a digital PSA about the benefits of life insurance with mortgage protection. Every post that highlights this message or email that encapsulates this message advances a cause for the good. And every advancement due to this message is an act of goodness.

In writing this message, insurers have the potential to underwrite more life insurance policies with mortgage protection.

*

"Life is constantly providing us with new funds, new resources, even when we are reduced to immobility. In life's ledger there is no such thing as frozen assets."

—Henry Miller

As to the size of the private credit market, we agree with Blackstone_Credit[281]: The market is still relatively small, representing $1.2 trillion[282] or 30 percent of overall credit markets.

Through revolving lines of credit, backed by a diverse pool of receivables, we limit risk and contain volatility.

As most asset-based loans cover short-term expenses, the loans serve as "transactional funding" for operations, acquisitions, capital improvements, and cash flow.

As most asset-based loans reflect different levels of risk, the loans charge different interest rates.

As Mandel ABL Fund LP has different levels of risk tolerance, we have a finite amount of downside risk.

*

"Alone we can do so little. Together we can do so much."

—Helen Keller

Deeds to property are like titles to works: a chance for real estate agents and insurers to come together. In doing so, they may offer life insurance with mortgage protection to homeowners, for the good of all homeowners.

The proof is not only on a piece of paper but in the peace of mind homeowners enjoy. The benefit is in knowing that loss of property will not follow loss of life, that devastation among the living will not follow burial of the dead, that foreclosure will not follow the need

281 "Private Credit's Rapid Growth: A Secular Trend." *Blackstone*, April 2022, www.bcred.com/wp-content/uploads/sites/11/2020/10/Private-Credits-Rapid-Growth_A-Secular-Trend.pdf?v=1649296149

282 Mac Eochaidh, Treabhor. "Private debt: global market opportunities." *Preqin*, 19 July 2022, www.preqin.com/insights/research/blogs/private-debt-global-market-opportunities

for closure. We can eliminate the fear of foreclosure by deputizing real estate agents, thus making them advocates of life insurance or insurance agents outright.

Either way, everyone wins. Real estate agents earn additional income, insurers underwrite additional policies, and homeowners receive additional protection.

Failure to communicate is the cause of our problem. And when no one communicates, no one wins.

But before we can get real estate agents to talk to homeowners, we must set our own house in order. We must recognize that practice is a prerequisite to preaching, just as attentiveness is a perquisite of having a calling, of answering the call to spread the word. We must do as we say, and we must have something to say. We must replace silence with words of soundness, thus converting a stutter of hesitancy into a score of certainty and turning applause into action.

The proof is in the freedom—the freedoms—real estate agents and insurers can deliver.

The proof is in freedom from fear of foreclosure.

The proof is in freedom from want, allowing families the financial strength to live.

The proof is in the freedom to recover, giving homeowners the added value of time.

Time to grieve permits time to rest. Time to heal permits time to learn. And time to think permits time to do. Preaching the value of time is a virtue. Adopting this value guarantees continuity, and applying this guarantee secures the value of a family's greatest asset.

Real estate agents and insurers share these values. And home-owners deserve the protection these values afford.

CHAPTER 10

Securing Excellence

"A truly American sentiment recognizes the dignity of labor and the fact that honor lies in honest toil."

—Grover Cleveland

All labor has dignity, according to a King's[283] paean to a street sweeper. Thus does the speaker say:

Sweep streets like Michelangelo painted pictures. Sweep streets like Beethoven composed music. Sweep streets like Shakespeare wrote poetry.

The call to have a calling, the call to discover what we are called to do, that is the purpose of life and the meaning of work. And the call to employers is an admonition to recognize that what furthers the soul does not feed the body, and that spiritual recompense is not a dispensation from the laws governing labor.

Worker retention should be every employer's job. After all, every job is just and the desire for just compensation is no dream. If

[283] The Martin Luther King, Jr. Center for Nonviolent Social Change. (2015, July 6). *MLK: What Is Your Life's Blueprint?* [Video]. YouTube. https://youtu.be/kmsAxX84cjQ

employers want assurances from workers that they will not leave their jobs, life insurance is a solution for management and labor. It levels the scales of competition, allowing employers to retain talent without bankrupting themselves in the process.

Because of the flexibility life insurance offers, employers can write and underwriters can issue policies that appeal to workers. These policies address the needs of specific workers by honoring workers through a combination of words and actions. And the benefits are as diverse as any policy of workplace diversity.

In other words, deeds make real the promises of a deed or a contract.

If, for example, an employer wants to introduce a deferred compensation plan and retain workers, awarding tax-free bonuses that mature within a set timeframe, indexed universal life (IUL) insurance[284] expedites this plan.

The advantages of an IUL policy include:

- Financial security for a worker's family and loved ones
- The upside potential of a bull market
- Downside protection from market losses and the severity of a bear market
- Access to the potential cash value of the portfolio
- Additional options for employers and/or workers

To make these advantages available to workers *and* increase the probability that employers will introduce an IUL policy with these advantages—that takes communication.

---

[284] "Indexed universal life insurance." *Lincoln Financial Group*, www.lincolnfinancial.com/public/individuals/products/lifeinsurance/permanentlife/indexeduniversallife

As to what employers say to workers, let the dialogue begin. Let both parties address facts in evidence, and let both parties have an open dialogue about the best possible solution.

*

"Dignity is as essential to human life as water, food, and oxygen."
—Lauren Hillenbrand, *Unbroken: A World War II Story of Survival, Resilience and Redemption*

When 97 percent of employers say they feel responsible for employee financial wellness, or when 91 percent of employers say offering more resources to manage financial wellness improves employee satisfaction, the message is clear. And when 46 percent of workers have resigned from their jobs over the past year, the result is a mass protest—a mass walkout—without a strike.

When Bank of America[285] (BofA) and the BBC[286] report on the same problem, names do not matter. Whether the term is the Great Resignation or the Great Reshuffle, the problem is serious and the effects severe. The *Monthly Labor Review*[287] (*MLR*)—the principal journal of the U.S. Bureau of Labor Statistics—says, "The pace of resignations seems to have risen more quickly than one would have expected from labor market tightening alone."

The BofA report gets to the essence of the present crisis, with 62 percent of employees saying they worry about their finances. And the chief worry for 80 percent of employees is inflation, with 71

285 "2022 Workplace Benefits Report: Navigating a new era of financial wellness." *Bank of America*, https://business.bofa.com/content/dam/flagship/workplace-benefits/id20_0901/documents/2022-WBR.pdf

286 Morgan, Kate. "Why workers just won't stop quitting." *BBC*, 18 August 2022, www.bbc.com/worklife/article/20220817-why-workers-just-wont-stop-quitting

287 "The 'Great Resignation' in perspective." *Monthly Labor Review*, July 2022, www.bls.gov/opub/mlr/2022/article/the-great-resignation-in-perspective.htm

percent saying the cost of living outpaces growth in their salary or wages.

The performance of the stock market does not lessen this worry—not when the average 401(k) balance is down 20 percent[288] from a year ago, or when the authors of an article in the *Yale Law Journal*[289] say 401(k) fees are so high that they "consume the tax benefits of investing in a 401(k) for a young employee."

More worrisome is the fact that, based on a survey by TD Ameritrade[290], 37 percent of 401(k) investors think they do not pay any fees while 22 percent do not know if their plan has fees. An additional 14 percent of investors say they do not know how to determine the fees.

"While often overlooked, fees can put a drag on investment performance and impact portfolio value over the long term," says Matthew Sadowsky, director of retirement and annuities at TD Ameritrade.

To James Kwak,[291] Jesse Root Professor of Law Emeritus at the University of Connecticut School of Law, the fees represent the

---

288 Press release. "Fidelity® Q2 2022 Retirement Analysis: Even With Market & Economic Uncertainty, Retirement Savers Look Long Term and Continue to Save." *Fidelity*, 17 August 2022, https://newsroom.fidelity.com/press-releases/news-details/2022/Fidelity-Q2-2022-Retirement-Analysis-Even-With-Market--Economic-Uncertainty-Retirement-Savers-Look-Long-Term-and-Continue-to-Save/default.aspx

289 Ayers, Ian and Quinn Curtis. "Beyond Diversification: The Pervasive Problem of Excessive Fees and 'Dominated Funds' in 401(k) Plans." *Yale Law Journal*, vol. 124, no. 5, March 2015, www.yalelawjournal.org/article/excessive-fees-and-dominated-funds-in-401k-plans

290 Press release. "Three-Quarters of Americans Are in the Dark When it Comes to 401(k) Fees." *Business Wire*, 29 January 2018, www.businesswire.com/news/home/20180129005124/en/Three-Quarters-of-Americans-Are-in-the-Dark-When-it-Comes-to-401-k-Fees

291 Kwak, James. "Improving Retirement Savings Options for Employees." *U. of Pennsylvania Journal of Business Law*, vol. 15, no. 2, March 2013, www.law.upenn.edu/live/files/1804-kwak15upajbusl4832013pdf

siphoning off of tens of billions of dollars every year. Kwak repeats the question A.C. Pritchard[292] of the University of Michigan Law School asks, regarding the widespread belief that it is possible to beat the market.

"Because the financial services industry requires these myths for its very existence," Pritchard says, "if investors were to switch en masse to index funds and other forms of passive investment, the Wall Street-industrial complex would crumble."

Pritchard's assertion is clear. But the impact of his assertion is unclear.

Unless the impact is the end of a movement in progress—and unless we cannot hear the sound of millions of 401(k) investors moving their money elsewhere—I believe the impact will be quiet and meaningless.

That's not to say I disagree with Pritchard. On the contrary, I second his assertion. I believe what he says. And I speak his language, for we speak the same language about the nature of Wall Street and the nature of human nature.

Were he to revise and extend his remarks, naming the captives who speak for their employers and do not speak freely, I would applaud the thoroughness and truth of his remarks. Were Pritchard to add all agents who speak in accordance with the law and in violation of the laws of conscience and fair play, I would commend him.

To Pritchard's main point about what workers believe about the stock market, allow me to say what I know about work and the labor market. Because work is fluid and workers are mobile, the nature of work is as dynamic as the seasons and as unpredict-

---

[292] Pritchard, Adam C. "The SEC at 70: Time for Retirement?" *Notre Dame Law Review*, vol. 80, no. 3, 2005, https://repository.law.umich.edu/cgi/viewcontent.cgi?article=1508&context=articles

able as the weather. What *is* predictable is what a life insurance policy does, when it takes effect, how much it pays, and to whom it applies.

What is also predictable is the need among employers to retain their most valuable workers. By this standard, the face value of a life insurance policy is not the total value of a life insurance policy—not when a policy yields dividends by boosting loyalty and improving morale.

But here again a policy of best practice in business is nothing without practice in the art of communication. This truth works to answer the concerns of employers. For them, two questions are paramount:

1. Why invest in recruiting and training workers when someone else can profit from this investment?
2. Why hire anyone when there is no way to stop everyone from joining another employer?

Both questions speak to matters of risk and to that which is containable but unavoidable. And both questions are reducible to a single question: What should employers do about uncertainty?

In so many words: deal with it.

The onus is on the financial translator to tell employers the facts about life insurance. Doing so is not expensive—though any such expense is defensible—because the price of success is responsibility. And the responsibility to inform is a price all parties should acknowledge, because it is the financial translator's duty to explain everything in advance.

If workers want to maximize their worth, they should be party to this presentation.

If employers want to lower risk, they should present workers with the certainty life insurance provides.

If insurers want to expand their influence and have a positive impact on society, they should have a financial translator who can liaison with employers and communicate with workers.

The responsibility to lead is a price employers should accept.

By any standard, life insurance works to the benefit of employers and workers.

*

"He found something that he wanted, had always wanted and always would want—not to be admired, as he had feared; not to be loved, as he had made himself believe; but to be necessary to people, to be indispensable ..."
—F. Scott Fitzgerald, *This Side of Paradise*

As important as worker retention is, life after the death of an employer is no less important. And the key to a worker's livelihood is keyperson insurance[293].

Also known as key person insurance, the policy is a form of business life insurance. The beneficiary is the business itself, should an owner or executive who is critical to the life of the business die. The business also pays the premiums.

The value is in the protection the policy provides for a business, so the loss of one is not a loss for all who work to keep a business alive. The value is in the preservation of a person's work, so the work may go on and the memory of the founder may never die.

---

293 "What is key person insurance?" *Nationwide Mutual Insurance Company*, www.nationwide.com/lc/resources/investing-and-retirement/articles/what-is-key-person-insurance

The value is in having the means to hire a person to keep a business in business.

We are, after all, a nation of small business owners. A nation, in fact, in which small businesses account for 99.9 percent of all businesses in the U.S.

We have 32.5 million small businesses throughout the U.S. Small businesses also account for 65.1 percent of net new job creation since 2000, according to the Small Business Administration (SBA[294]). This percentage translates to 1.5 million new jobs per year.

Because of these statistics, lenders may mandate that a business purchase key person insurance. The same is true for investors, considering their investment is often in the person who writes the algorithm or patents the product that changes how we live.

Not every business survives the loss of a leader or death of a founder. But every business has a right to know how to save itself from an otherwise irrevocable loss. The financial translator is indispensable to this process. He does his job, and every job[295] counts, regardless of what happens.

Should the worst happen, key person insurance may be vital to what happens next. Without it, the worst may be more than a business can withstand.

---

294 "Frequently Asked Questions About Small Businesses." *Office of Advocacy, U.S. Small Business Administration*, October 2020, https://cdn.advocacy.sba.gov/wp-content/uploads/2020/11/05122043/Small-Business-FAQ-2020.pdf

295 Richard Nixon Foundation. (2012, January 16). *President Nixon's Farewell to the White House Staff* [Video]. YouTube. https://youtu.be/32GaowQnGRw

CHAPTER 11

The Need for Speed

"In skating over thin ice our safety is in our speed."
—Ralph Waldo Emerson, *The Collected Works*

From delay born of pandemic to decisiveness borne by leaders with a plan, from anger born of isolation to action borne by people's refusal to isolate themselves from the world, the authors of the first chapter of our post-pandemic life—the writers of this history—are the underwriters of life insurance.

The men and women responsible for the expansion of accelerated underwriting deserve their place in history. The public has a right to know, and the insurance industry has a duty to promote, what accelerated underwriting is. They should know that new technologies make it fast and affordable to review life insurance applications; that insurers can check prescriptions, driving records, and all relevant records in minutes; that this process is safe and noninvasive, free of undergoing a physical or having someone enter a physical premise.

Because of a combination of timing and technology, accelerated underwriting is no longer an option for the few. In our modern world, it may soon become a preference of the many. And for these reasons and many more, including the need to slow or stop the spread of COVID-19, accelerated underwriting may save lives while increasing sales of life insurance. But people cannot buy what they do not know exists.

People need to know that eligibility does not depend on electability. They must realize they do not have to elect to put themselves at risk to have insurers assess the risks of issuing life insurance.

What is available online avails insurers the opportunity to earn the trust of consumers. Sustaining this trust is what accelerates how consumers can create trusts or tax-free income, thanks to owning life insurance. And what makes this trust possible in the first place is accelerated underwriting.

The terms may differ—the terms *do* differ—but the conditions are the same. Accelerated underwriting is not conditioned on strangers visiting applicants' homes. Matters of personal health are a matter of public health, such that people of a certain age or condition do not want to increase their vulnerability or lower their immunity to illness.

Put another way—no one wants to die *from* life insurance, but many want to die *with* life insurance.

Accelerated underwriting is true to its name. It uses technology to collect and analyze data. From there, insurers can determine specific costs for specific consumers. The process is efficient and economical for everyone, allowing insurers to write more policies while enabling consumers to compare prices.

But again, where the process of moving faster slows is where the act of communication fails to start.

The act of translating industry data, of setting and surpassing goals, of separating what matters to insurers and what should matter to consumers, this act—as it relates to a one-page presentation from the National Association of Insurance Commissioners

(NAIC[296])—is an effort to help the public understand the importance of accelerated underwriting.

The process is not foreign to the insurance industry. After all, close to 90 percent[297] of life insurers use or plan to use automated underwriting techniques. And as the tools and techniques of accelerated underwriting expand, the need to translate the value of accelerated underwriting expands too.

Accelerated underwriting is a universal good, based on the good of intelligence, for the purchase of goods in the form of life insurance. The result serves the common good, strengthening individuals and families. For this good to flourish, acts of goodness demand swift and secure action.

Now is the time to accelerate the use of accelerated underwriting. In doing so, we may speed up the day when all who want life insurance can have it.

*

"Character is much easier kept than recovered."
—Thomas Paine

Life insurance policies abound. But policies that insure a person despite the absence of bodily harm—that exist because of the threat of reputational harm and that ease the degree of harm—are hard to find.

These policies are also expensive, regardless of whether a person is rich and famous. And these policies are a necessity for people

---

[296] PowerPoint Presentation: LIMRA Underwriting for NAIC Big Data WG 2018-08-04 (Slide 2) [PowerPoint slides]. Retrieved from NAIC: https://content.naic.org/sites/default/files/inline-files/LIMRA%20Underwriting%20for%20NAIC%20Big%20Data%20WG%202018-08-04%20%28002%29.pptx

[297] "Accelerated Underwriting." *Center for Insurance Policy and Research*, 14 June 2022, https://content.naic.org/cipr-topics/accelerated-underwriting

at the commanding heights of society, because no one has total command of what anyone can do to a person's reputation.

As captives of chance, we have the chance to benefit from captive insurance. We have recourse from the infliction of harm.

As an alternative to traditional commercial insurance, captives participate in the alternative risk transfer (ART) market.

Because of this alternative, captives risk their own capital. They accept the risks of forming their own insurance companies, of having parent groups create these companies for them. This way, they may avoid volatile pricing and difficulties in purchasing the policies they want. And by developing bespoke policies, captives can reduce costs, increase cash flow, write policies, set premiums, and return or reinvest unused funds.

As a specific type of insurance and an example of insurance thought leadership, captive insurance makes sense. However, these policies are rare. That is not to say these policies do not exist—but when available, they tend to originate from offshore insurers.

More common are deductible reimbursement policies, where companies increase deductibles with their respective carriers.

Captives assume the risk of paying deductibles when they file a claim with traditional carriers.

As history proves and as a footnote to history confirms, vandals would replace a life of service with headlines from a person's time as a public servant. The death of Raymond

J. Donovan[298], labor secretary in the Reagan administration, underscores this point.

Just as vindication in a court of law is no shield from vilification via the court of public opinion, an acquittal is no guarantee of absolution from the influencers of public opinion. And just as justice is blind to the injustice of Donovan's ordeal, the world is deaf to his post-trial plea:

"Which office do I go to to get my reputation back?"

Donovan's question was rhetorical then, but it need not be—it should not be—now. Certainly not when anonymous forces can harm a person's reputation in seconds. Not when outrageous lies can exhaust a person's fortune. And not when it can be a person's misfortune to see his life's work collapse in real time.

Consider the online implications of reputational harm, where damaging content costs the consumer market in the U.S. $537 billion[299] in business.

Consider these takeaways from the 2022 Edelman Connected Crisis Study[300]:

- Crisis management is the fastest-growing area of responsibility for CCOs and CMOs.
- Companies continue to underestimate the expectation to engage on societal issues.

---

[298] Fried, Joseph P. "Raymond Donovan, 90, Dies; Labor Secretary Quit Under a Cloud." *New York Times*, 5 June 2021, www.nytimes.com/2021/06/05/us/raymond-j-donovan-dead.html?smid=nytcore-ios-share&referringSource=articleShare

[299] Winfrey, Graham. "The Cost of Unhappy Customers." *Inc.*, 7 July 2014, www.inc.com/graham-winfrey/the-cost-of-unhappy-customers.html

[300] "2022 Connected Crisis Study: In search of stability amidst chaos." *Edelman*, www.edelman.com/sites/g/files/aatuss191/files/2022-09/2022%20Edelman%20Connected%20Crisis%20Study.pdf

- Businesses are missing the mark on how to protect themselves in times of crisis.
- Companies must demonstrate a deep understanding of cultural nuances, local customs, and community interests.

Insurance from reputational harm may be the only way to ensure loss of livelihood does not lead to loss of life, that character assassination does not lead to self-harm, and that a leader does not commit suicide.

Unless a public figure has this insurance—or knows that captive insurance is a means of buying this insurance—reputational harm can be hurtful. In fact, it can be so hurtful as to be harmful to the survival of the body politic and the success of the nation.

The enemies of freedom want first-rate leaders to not put their country first. They want leaders to sacrifice the right to choose in the first place. They want our leaders to lose their sacred honor. And if the enemy succeeds in their attempts, then America as a nation loses.

We must not lose. We will not lose.

CHAPTER 12

The Impact of PPLI: Private Placement Life Insurance

"PPLI is one of the greatest investment products out there for those who want to protect their money from unnecessary taxation and leave it for future generations."

—Jonathan Feldman

Wealth is the product of work itself. And whether that product is a wealth of money or a wealth of deeds for which money advances good deeds, protecting wealth from excess taxation is essential.

Private placement[301] life insurance (PPLI) is protection that accredited investors with a minimum net worth of $1 million (excluding their primary residence), or income of at least $200,000 in each of the preceding two years, should have. Accredited investors, including married couples with income of $300,000 in each of the preceding two years, should also have PPLI.

Requirements differ among foreign-based PPLI carriers, while modified endowment contract (MEC) regulations ensure that pol-

---

[301] "Private Placement Life Insurance." *Geneva International*, https://genevappli.com/products/

icies have the same tax advantages as U.S.-based life insurance contracts.

With PPLI, which is available to accredited investors, the advantages are:

- Access to advisers who provide clear and thorough information on the complexity of PPLI structures
- A range of customizable PPLI products (based on a client's financial needs and goals)
- Support from a global network of insurance, legal, accounting, and investment professionals
- The freedom to keep an existing life insurance policy and place it inside a PPLI structure

Without the protection PPLI offers, and based on the Biden administration's plan to raise the estate tax, the wealth of generations borne by many over the course of decades or centuries will now go to the government.

With the protection PPLI offers, an accredited investor can buy a variable universal life insurance policy to safeguard or increase his wealth. So long as the domestic investor can pay a minimum amount of annual premiums for four years, in addition to maintaining enough cash value to cover the cost of insurance, PPLI offers an investor a wealth of options. These include tax-free benefits to an heir(s) and tax-eliminated growth of the investments that make up the cash value inside the policy.

Also, the policy owner often can access funds, tax-free, through policy loans and up to basis withdrawals. And because the insured assigns ownership to another individual or to an Irrevocable Life Insurance Trust (ILIT)[302], the policy is not part of the taxable estate. Provided the cash value is not zero, thus causing the pol-

[302] "Irrevocable Life Insurance Trust (ILIT)." *Legal Information Institute*, March 2022, www.law.cornell.edu/wex/irrevocable_life_insurance_trust_(ilit)

icy to lapse, PPLI is a convenient and customizable source of protection for an accredited investor.

These advantages more than offset any administrative costs. The insured can create a diversified portfolio of insurance dedicated funds (IDFs) charged with managing the assets of the policy.

For example, the cash value in a contract may be invested in an IDF that only manages money for life insurance policy cash accounts. Other IDFs offer private equity funds, commodity funds, funds of hedge funds, real estate investment trusts (REITs), and venture capital investments.

The PPLI must, however, meet IRS rules pertaining to investor control, insurance, and diversification. Professional administrators of the cash value to ensure compliance are a necessary requirement. Working with approved registered investment advisors to manage that cash value in compliant, and approved investment solutions via these managed accounts is a newer option for policy owners. No policy owner can control the cash value in the policy without the investor control rules being violated.

By working with a knowledgeable PPLI insurance adviser, the insured can best select these registered money managers to oversee individual investments within a portfolio. Choosing multiple managers can mitigate risk, just as having a diversified portfolio can reduce volatility. Cash value must be diversified into at least five different investments with no more than 55 percent in any one investment, 70 percent in any two investments, 80 percent in any three investments, and 90 percent in any four investments.

Choice of registered asset managers is the foundation of PPLI investing, as accredited investors want to maintain their financial freedom. Doing so gives them the means to perpetuate a legacy, promote a cause, or preserve a lifetime of service. They may do as they please, in accord with their ideals, on behalf of a universal ideal. And that freedom is true and righteous altogether.

Protecting wealth protects the freedom of one to help many.

Protecting the few who are wealthy increases opportunities for the many to build wealth.

Protecting what wealth makes possible protects what the wealthy can make probable: charity for those who need it, education for those who crave it, culture for those who cherish it.

PPLI is the protection the wealthy deserve, so they can strengthen what they can give.

*

"Death is not the end; there remains the litigation over the estate."

—Ambrose Bierce, *The Collected Works*

Things as certain as death and taxes can be firmly believed. Also believable is the fact that life is volatile and that the cost of living is highly variable.

For these reasons and more, protecting your estate from taxation is why life insurance exists. How you structure this protection—transferring ownership of your policy and ensuring the payment of premiums while excluding this asset from your estate—is critical.

That you act is critical, as the Biden administration wants to change major portions of the estate tax. To start, the Tax Cuts and

Jobs Act[303] (TCJA) of 2017 exempts estates worth up to $11.7 million.

Whether life insurance proceeds are part of the taxable estate depends on who owns the policy at the time of the insured's death. If you want to preserve your legacy, the owner and beneficiary of the proceeds from your life insurance policy must be another person or legal entity. Remember to choose wisely, because the owner of the policy is the person who is responsible for maintaining the policy.

Because you do not want the policy to lapse due to failure on the owner's part—or if the owner is a minor who is not able to pay the premiums without the approval of a legal guardian or trustee—make sure procedures are in place to make ownership convenient and secure.

An irrevocable life insurance trust (ILIT) is another means to a similar end, regarding estates and specific tax thresholds. In this case, the policy is owned by a trust. The proceeds are not part of your estate, nor are you a trustee in charge of the trust. You also do not retain any rights to run or revoke the trust.

The advantage here is the assurance that what must be done will be done. Premiums will be paid without delay, and the trust will honor its legal responsibilities.

An estate planning adviser can also determine if you can transfer money—funds relating to gifts—to the trust, thus reducing whatever taxes your estate may owe. If the beneficiary is a child or an adult with special needs, an ILIT lets you name the trustee—a person you trust—to whom you entrust the handling of money on

---

[303] H.R.1 – 115th Congress (2017-2019): Tax Cuts and Jobs Act, H.R.1, 115th Cong. (2017), www.congress.gov/115/bills/hr1/BILLS-115hr1enr.pdf

behalf of your child or children, according to the terms of the trust document.

In a word, documentation is key to any estate plan. Documentation is verification of trust, affording you the peace of mind you deserve. Regardless of who owns the policy—whether the owner is an individual or an institution such as a legal trust—proof is in the paperwork. In other words, legal documentation is proof of ownership.

Do not linger in attending to this work, lest the government be fastidious in taxing the proceeds of your estate. Trust, too, that the government will tax your estate unless you safeguard it.

For the good of your estate, with the opportunity for future generations to continue to do good, do what is right. Exercise the rights life insurance provides.

CHAPTER 13
Windfall

"As yet, the wind is an untamed, and unharnessed force; and quite possibly one of the greatest discoveries hereafter to be made, will be the taming, and harnessing of the wind."
—Abraham Lincoln

Lincoln's words resound with the precision of science and the power of scripture. But they do not describe how we live now.

We live as dependents, reliant on an infrastructure—an electrical grid[304]—that has more miles of cable than tracks of rail or road, and which stretches across states without strengthening the independence of the United States.

The cables run between transmission towers. The towers stand as truss or lattice towers of steel. They stand as pylons, like "The Pylons"[305] in verse, rising above the hamlets and hills of the countryside. These towers are rusting throughout the country, with

---

304 McLaughlin, Tim. "Creaky U.S. power grid threatens progress on renewables, EVs." *Reuters*, 12 May 2022, www.reuters.com/investigates/special-report/usa-renewables-electric-grid/

305 Spender, Stephen. "The Pylons." *Allpoetry.com*, 1933, https://allpoetry.com/The-Pylons

many lying twisted and torn, in the aftermath of hurricanes and floods.

The towers stand like derricks, as the resemblance between the two evokes the landscape of the past.

As for the cables, which droop or sag for miles, the catenary shape is an effect of gravity and tension. The effect on the viewer, meanwhile—the effect on my viewpoint inside the cabin of my car—tends toward the catastrophic.

We have a grid overrun by a combination of nature, demand, and neglect. A grid that is far from green, which reminds me of the drive through Green Valley, California, where the Sierra Pelona Mountains are dry and brown, and the area is prone to brownouts and rolling blackouts.

Such a system is not only unsustainable—it is unable to provide sustainable energy.

This system cannot survive in its present state. Not in California nor any other state with a Zero-Emission Vehicle[306] (ZEV) program. If California is the America of America, one must drive the

[306] "Zero-Emission Vehicle Program." *California Air Resources Board*, https://ww2.arb.ca.gov/our-work/programs/zero-emission-vehicle-program

freeways of the Golden State and take the Golden State Freeway, Interstate 5 (I-5), to read[307] America in the original.

Driving anywhere in America is necessary to understand the nature of America, and the power available from nature, per my time behind the wheel. Driving on I-4, outside Celebration, Florida, the stylized pylon shines white as traffic heads toward Walt Disney World. A loop with two smaller adjoining loops, the Mickey pylon[308]—five miles from Cinderella Castle and Magic Kingdom Park—stands like a pillar with a trio of Olympic rings.

Past shades of blue and pink, past the castle's bold colors and the lights of Spaceship Earth, past the "Beacons of Magic" and the burst of fireworks, night returns and the darkness of reality resumes.

The hexagonal trusses disappear, and the triangular patterns fade from view.

---

307 Banham, Reyner. (2009). *Los Angeles: The Architecture of Four Ecologies*. University of California Press. www.ucpress.edu/book/9780520260153/los-angeles

308 Mickey Pylon Photo: Mickey (3153436441) [Photograph]. Retrieved from Wikimedia Commons: https://en.wikipedia.org/wiki/Mickey_pylon#/media/File%3AMickey_(3153436441).jpg

The geodesic dome of EPCOT Center vanishes as Future World[309] no longer exists.

Modern life looks nothing like Uncle Walt's community of tomorrow, what with the inefficiency and waste of our electrical grid. And yet, solutions whirl about continually, just as the wind comes again on its circuit, making offshore wind[310] a potentially lucrative investment.

To meet the world's desire to protect our planet, most green energy strategies will not be enough. We will eventually embrace nuclear energy as no other solution is possible.

---

[309] Michaelsen, Shannen, "Future World Is No More, 'Neighborhoods' Have Now Replaced 1972 Land at EPCOT." *WDW News Today*, 27 September 2021, https://wdwnt.com/2021/09/new-neighborhoods-debut-at-epcot/

[310] "Offshore Wind Research and Development." *Office of Energy Efficiency & Renewable Energy*, www.energy.gov/eere/wind/offshore-wind-research-and-development

For an investor with a guaranteed source of tax-free income, exposure to a variety of alternative energy investments has the potential to boost their overall return and reduce volatility.

*

"Disorganization can scarcely fail to result in efficiency."

—Dwight D. Eisenhower

The pylons[311] look best in Abilene, Kansas, where they line the background of the Dwight D. Eisenhower Presidential Library, Museum & Boyhood Home.

Before them, in the foreground, stands a bronze statue of the general in uniform. Here, where the pylons number five and match the number of inscriptions on the base of the statue, stands an icon of service and a warrior for peace. Here, where each pylon commemorates a milestone in the life of a soldier and statesman, the father of the Interstate Highway System also rests.

Here, in this town of the grassy plain, the sign for I-70 reads like an affirmation of the psalm. The highway approaches its allotment of threescore years and ten, because the highway is (at the time of writing) sixty-six years old.

The highway and the system to which it belongs is in disrepair.

The system is not true to the cherished ideals of true democracy for which the pylons stand, upon which the words say, "Each American works in his daily task at plough or forge or machine or desk knowing this nation will forever stand one and indivisible in devotion to the cause of liberty for all mankind."

---

[311] "About Us." *Dwight D. Eisenhower Presidential Library, Museum & Boyhood Home*, www.eisenhowerlibrary.gov/about-us

The system summons us to increase our devotion to the work of this great man, General Eisenhower, whose home[312] stands outside a great battlefield; whose works on war and remembrance, the volumes recounting a mandate for change and a crusade to wage peace, bear Eisenhower's voice; whose works speak to us still, in Gettysburg, Pennsylvania.

By improving the system and repairing the breach, we help ourselves by helping our country. The profits are in the words of the prophet, for what the twelfth verse of the fifty-eighth chapter says, the paths show that U.S. Route 58 is a threat in the east and State Route 58 a disaster in the west; that we have foundations to raise and roads to restore; that we have places to be and things to build.

The impact is in investing well.

*

"Wind power is widely seen as the source of renewable energy with the best chance of competing with fossil-fuel power stations in the near term."

—*The Economist*

The pylon looks like a Parisian in Provence and a Texan in France. Because this pylon—the truss tower outside Love Civic Center—is a scale model of the Eiffel Tower in Paris, France.

The model[313] wears a red cowboy hat and stands sixty-five feet tall in Paris, Texas. Here, where the city has no highway connect-

---

312 "Ike, Gettysburg, and the Cold War." *National Park Service*, 6 January 2023, www.nps.gov/eise/index.htm

313 Acosta, Zoee. "You Can Visit This Giant Eiffel Tower In Paris, Texas." *NARCITY Magazine*, 3 April 2019, www.paristexas.com/eiffel-tower/

ing to an interstate highway, a model of 3D wind-power[314] technology stands in Northeast Texas.

The working model has the power to outproduce a nuclear power plant on the same area of land. The model is further proof of which way the wind blows, as I go from the Lone Star State to the Hawkeye State, and explore Walnut, Iowa, and the Walnut Wind Farm[315].

The farm is modern while all the town is a stage.

Here, in Iowa's Antique City, where the painting features the ghost in a ghost sign, a temptress teases the tagline[316]: Drink Coca-Cola from a Bottle Through a Straw.

Here, among the hitching posts and vintage streetlights, the town's 739 residents play many parts.

Here and elsewhere, wind turbines generate 58 percent[317] of Iowa's electricity.

The opportunity for the next generation of wind investors is for offshore wind power generation. Land near power grids and near the ocean will be the most sought-after real estate in the coming years. Offshore wind energy needs to be delivered onshore, and its power must be fed into our grid system.

---

314 "East Texas inventor concentrating on wind power technology." *Associated Press*, 16 August 2019, https://myparistexas.com/east-texas-inventor-concentrating-on-wind-power-technology/

315 Eric Woerth. (2021). *Walnut Wind Farm* [Video]. Vimeo. https://vimeo.com/479969966

316 Google Search Image: [Image]. Retrieved from Google Images: https://www.traveliowa.com/userdocs/cities/16o_Roberts_Bakery3_Walnut_KTitus-custom.jpg

317 "U.S Energy Atlas with Total Energy Layers." *EIA*, 21 July 2022, www.eia.gov/state/?sid=IA

Battery storage sites contiguous to the grid will certainly be in high demand as well.

*

"As the saying goes, the Stone Age did not end because we ran out of stones; we transitioned to better solutions. The same opportunity lies before us with energy efficiency and clean energy."

—Steven Chu

The wind carries me to a valley of light in the Silver State, home of the Copper Mountain Solar Complex[318].

Here, in the Great Basin of the Mojave Desert, the panels look like an oasis—a blue waterway—in a sea of gravel and sand. Across the flatness of earth and hardness of rock, the panels convert light into electricity. Across five facilities and 4,000 acres, the panels rank in rows and tilt from east to west.

The panels bring the lights to the City of Lights, where the Welcome to Fabulous Las Vegas sign is a diamond-shaped beacon and the Las Vegas Strip is a four-mile-long display of LED lights.

The lights color the Eiffel Tower at Paris Las Vegas red, green, and gold. The half-scale replica of the real thing stands 540 feet tall, a truss tower alongside canals in which gondoliers sing and fountains dance, and where a pyramid projects the strongest beam of light in the world.

Here, where the streets form a grid and the Strip looks like a runway at night, the panels bring the city to life. They shine a light on the fact that, according to a study by international anal-

---

318 "Copper Mountain Solar III." *QBE*, 2018-2019, www.qbe.com/premiums4good/investment-highlights/copper-mountain-solar-iii

ysis group Wood Mackenzie[319], creating a majority renewables electrical grid will:

- Deploy over $1 trillion in capital investment over the next decade
- Support nearly 1 million direct, renewable energy jobs
- Reduce U.S. carbon emissions by over 60 percent

Wood Mackenzie says administrative action can accelerate the transition to renewable energy. And this point about action—that we need to improve and expand the grid—is a priority for America and an opportunity to benefit from investing in America.

The point is, "The country needs and, unless I mistake its temper, the country demands bold, persistent experimentation. It is common sense to take a method and try it: If it fails, admit it frankly and try another. But above all, try something."

Then New York Governor Franklin Delano Roosevelt[320] made this point on May 22, 1932, in his commencement address at Oglethorpe University.

FDR's point still stands. Or rather, the points stand as works of progress born of his administration, from Hoover Dam to the Triborough Bridge, from Chickamauga Dam to LaGuardia Airport, from New Orleans City Park to the Arroyo Seco Parkway.

*

---

319 "US renewable energy policy scenario analysis." *Wood Mackenzie,* 16 December 2020, www.woodmac.com/our-expertise/focus/Power--Renewables/us-renewable-energy-policy-scenario-analysis/

320 Aiken, Debbie. "Remembering FDR's Commencement Address at Oglethorpe." *The Source*, 22 May 2012, https://source.oglethorpe.edu/2012/05/22/remembering-fdrs-commencement-speech-at-oglethorpe/

"A life is not important except in the impact it has on other lives."

—Jackie Robinson

Jack Roosevelt Robinson, whose middle name honors the life of Theodore Roosevelt (TR), and whose achievements in life the nation honors, continues to impact the life of the nation. Born three weeks and four days after TR's death, Robinson made his Major League Baseball debut two days after the second anniversary of FDR's death.

Robinson's impact—as a soldier in uniform and as a Hall of Famer in Dodger blue—embodies FDR's description of the arsenal of democracy[321].

If we are to make an impact, we must apply ourselves with the same resolution, the same sense of urgency, and the same spirit of patriotism and sacrifice that Jackie Robinson or FDR would show were they with us.

The impact is in our dedication to the infrastructure of our democracy and the preservation of our shrines to freedom.

Among these works are the Jefferson Memorial, whose circular colonnade features twenty-six Ionic columns, and the Peristyle—the dancing pavilion—whose colonnade has thirty-six Ionic columns.

From these works we go forward together, for we are all Republicans or Democrats on our National System of Interstate and Defense Highways.

*

---

[321] Roosevelt, Franklin D. "The Arsenal of Democracy." *Franklin D. Roosevelt Presidential Library and Museum*, 29 December 1940, www.fdrlibraryvirtualtour.org/page07-06.asp

"Nuclear energy is incomparably greater than the molecular energy which we use today ... What is lacking is the match to set the bonfire alight."

—Winston Churchill

I cannot help reflecting on the foresight of this great man, whose last great speech to the House of Commons speaks to us still. His voice speaks for the great powers of the Old World and the New, and whose leadership speaks of our responsibility to greatness.

Reflecting on the rise of small nuclear power plants[322], I cannot help hearing the prescience of his voice.

---

[322] Hughes, Trevor. "A $4B nuclear power plant backed by Bill Gates and Warren Buffett is set for construction in Wyoming." *USA Today*, 16 November 2021, www.usatoday.com/story/news/nation/2021/11/16/warren-buffett-bill-gates-build-nuclear-power-plant-wyoming/8634699002/

Reflecting on the rise of star power on Earth, of a breakthrough in nuclear fusion[323], I cannot help listening to the brilliance of his voice.

Reflecting on the rise of alternative energy, I cannot help knowing that we will seek to play an active role in funding these exciting developments.

---

[323] Simon, Clea. "Why nuclear fusion is so exciting." *The Harvard Gazette*, 13 December 2022, https://news.harvard.edu/gazette/story/2022/12/why-nuclear-fusion-is-so-exciting/

CHAPTER 14

The Final Season of a Hero

"Jackie Robinson made his country and you and me and all of us a shade more free."

—Roger Kahn

Jackie Robinson died on October 24, 1972, at age 53. The immediate cause of death was a heart attack, his third, due to complications from diabetes.

The *New York Times*[324] story about his death reads like an inventory of illnesses, from the aforementioned series of heart attacks to near-total blindness to all manner of ailments.

The story is of a hero troubled in life and blessed in tributes following his death. The story of his life is one of physical pain, from arthritis to knee infections to diabetic nerve damage.

---

[324] Altman, Lawrence K. "Diabetes Is Called Basic Cause of Robinson's Death." *New York Times*, 29 October 1972, www.nytimes.com/1972/10/29/archives/diabetes-is-called-basic-cause-of-robinsons-death.html

His life is a lesson in the need to treat diabetes. For in the lifetime since Robinson's death, a half-century later, diabetes has become a national epidemic.

*

"I was born with a bad pancreas, and I could have been born with something a lot worse. I wasn't particularly lucky, but I wasn't particularly unlucky, either."

—Kathryn Ormsbee, *Lucky Few*

Insurers influence what people do. We see this when analyzing the lines between advertising insurance policies and adopting policies in support of a specific group of people. We see it in the difference between issuing life insurance for diabetics and rewarding people for lowering their risk of developing complications from diabetes. And we see it when looking at high premiums with few benefits and affordable premiums with good benefits.

If insurers move people to get moving and inspire diabetics to live more active lives, chance and choice can come together. Diabetics should have more than an opportunity to buy life insurance. They should have *a range* of opportunities when buying life insurance.

In a nation with 37.3 million[325] diabetics, of which I *was* one, the insurance industry has a duty to dispel confusion with clarity. In delivering separate messages for people with type 1 versus type 2 diabetes, the insurance industry can reverse years of doubt with a statement for the ages. They can offer hope for people in either group of a certain minimum age, so a tenth of all Americans can know the truth: that diabetes is not a point of permanent or temporary disqualification.

---

325 "Statistics About Diabetes." *American Diabetes Association*, 28 July 2022, https://diabetes.org/about-us/statistics/about-diabetes

While a minority of diabetics have life insurance, most diabetics believe they are uninsurable. This fact persists despite all facts to the contrary—not because of people's refusal to accept the truth, but because of insurers' failure to make the truth understandable.

The fact is that failure to communicate *is* communicable. What a person believes affects how a person feels, and silence among insurers serves to sanction self-destructive behavior among diabetics. Until this fact changes, more lives will end before threescore years and ten, spreading sorrow as the lost fly away.

Insurers can lessen the magnitude of this tragedy, thus increasing financial security for diabetics and strengthening health care for all. But doing so requires an economy of words and a wealth of repetition, which can turn a message about insurability—that diabetics can and should buy life insurance—into an inevitability. Taking these steps is requirement for the survival and success of America, too, because we can ill afford illness to consume the life of our economy.

We cannot allow 96 million[326] American adults with prediabetes to further sicken or suffer, to go blind before they go limp, to lose their limbs before they lose their lives.

We cannot afford to be unclear—not when diabetics work to live longer and long to retire with nontaxable income. Not when diabetics want to buy life insurance and want to better the lives of their loved ones. Not when insurers need to help diabetics and diabetics welcome help from insurers.

---

[326] "Prediabetes." *Centers for Disease Control and Prevention*, 21 December 2021, https://www.cdc.gov/diabetes/basics/prediabetes.html

Aware of the power of messaging, and able to promote awareness among the recipients of a particular message, the insurance industry can enrich the lives of diabetics.

Whether insurers save a hundred lives or a thousand, whether they save more lives in a month than in a year, they will save the lives of diabetics.

CHAPTER 15
Winning

"The stock market is filled with individuals who know the price of everything, but the value of nothing."

—Philip Fisher

The price of trying to outperform the stock market is constant performance. The contest favors the market, not the man in the arena—the man who fills the plaza—who fights the bull.

Take away the showmanship of the contest, and the salesmanship too, and what remains is an act. The performance may be grand and the choreography great, what with the capework and costumes—a light show of gold and silk embroidery, with a flourish of French and Spanish design—but theatricality is no substitute for truth.

After the performance ends and the crowd leaves, the outcome is clear. Either the matador wins or the bull, goaded but not gored, waits for his next victim.

And yet reality does not deter others from trying to conquer the bull.

Each has a plan too complex to explain. And yet each believes his plan—a map with a mountain range of price patterns—is accurate.

The route is the result, meaning investors who take the route or traders who use investors' money to travel the route will arrive at the right place. But when things go wrong, for inconsistency is the constant that governs performance, the performer—the hedge fund manager—blames the market. The lesson, then, is that the route is too erroneous to read, too exhausting to follow, and too expensive to fix.

Better to invest in diversified arbitrage, a fund of funds within a life insurance contract. Portfolio managers at top alternative investment[327] firms offer a superior record of performance. At Mandel Innovative Fund, we advise our investors to have exposure to several of these talented managers, all of whom have consistent track records during most market cycles.

Access to such a fund is a chance for accredited investors to increase their respective funds and realize superior returns.

To be clear, what is possible or even probable is not a guarantee of that which is profitable. In other words, past performance is not necessarily indicative of future results. But based on the performance and exclusivity of these funds, the opportunity to invest and the fact that new investors may invest is a milestone opportunity.

*

**"This defines entrepreneur and entrepreneurship—
the entrepreneur always searches for change,
responds to it, and exploits it as an opportunity."**

—Peter F. Drucker, *Innovation and Entrepreneurship: Practice and Principles*

---

327 "Alternative Investments Reimagined." *Crystal Capital Partners*, www.crystalfunds.com/?utm_source=GMBlisting&utm_medium=organic

Where there is growth, there is opportunity. And where there is opportunity for one, there is hope for all. The opportunity to create opportunities for communities in need of growth, to create jobs for residents of communities in need of work, and to create communities for a country in need of hope—is true and righteous altogether.

By offering these opportunities, insurance entrepreneurs do their part to be true to what our forefathers said on paper—that coming together can ensure domestic tranquility and form a more perfect union.

Because of the tax incentives Opportunity Zones provide, insurance entrepreneurs may use this tool to help underserved communities nationwide. A product of the Tax Cuts and Jobs Act of 2017[328], Opportunity Zones provide a tax incentive for investors to reinvest their unrealized capital gains into dedicated Opportunity Zone Funds.

A long-term commitment on behalf of low-income communities, Opportunity Zones are census tracts in all fifty states as well as American Samoa, Guam, the Northern Mariana Islands, Puerto Rico, and the Virgin Islands. These tracts are candidates for renewal, not only because of the wrongs of the past, but because of the urgency of the present. After all, the past is present among generations of residents of the same communities, where change is negative, investment nonexistent, and existence itself a nightmare of poverty, strife, and despair.

The zones allow an investor to defer capital gains taxes for up to five years. An investor may exclude 100% of long- or short-term capital gains tax[329] by investing in an Opportunity Fund within

---

[328] H.R.1 – 115th Congress (2017-2019): Tax Cuts and Jobs Act, H.R.1, 115th Cong. (2017), www.congress.gov/115/bills/hr1/BILLS-115hr1enr.pdf

[329] "Opportunity Zones: Frequently Asked Questions." *IRS.gov*, 10 November 2022, www.irs.gov/credits-deductions/opportunity-zones-frequently-asked-questions

180 days of the realization of that gain. After ten years, all capital gains on the investment in the Opportunity Zones are waived.

To qualify, the Opportunity Fund must invest more than 90 percent of its assets in a Qualified Opportunity Zone property or business located in an Opportunity Zone.

The property must be significantly improved, which means it must be an original use, or the basis of the property must be double the basis of the non-land assets. The business must also remain compliant as an Opportunity Zone-qualified company.

States may designate up to 25 percent of low-income census tracts as Opportunity Zones. To date, there are 8,764 Opportunity Zones[330] in the United States, many of which have experienced a lack of investment for decades.

*

"Do not cast me off in the time of old age; Do not forsake me when my strength fails."

—Psalms 71:9

The U.S. spent over $400 billion on long-term services and supports (LTSS) in 2020, according to the Congressional Budget Office (CBO[331]).

Medicaid paid $215 billion toward institutional and in-home care combined (or over half of all spending on LTSS).

---

[330] "Opportunity Zones," *U.S. Department of Housing and Urban Development*, https://opportunityzones.hud.gov/home

[331] "How CBO Analyzes the Costs of Proposals for Single-Payer Health Care Systems That Are Based on Medicare's Fee-for-Service Program." *Congressional Budget Office*, 10 December 2020, www.cbo.gov/publication/56811

The money in question is like the year in which the money was spent. Just because 20/20 is a term for visual acuity—just because the numbers overlap with the year—does not mean 2020 evokes memories of visionary leadership.

I have helped launch a company that seeks to prevent a repeat of a year of misrule and mourning, because where there is no vision, the people perish. Or rather, the people go poor before they perish due to the costs of long-term care.

Consider the following statistics from the Administration for Community Living (ACL[332]):

- Seventy percent of Americans turning sixty-five will need some type of long-term care in their remaining years.
- Women need care longer (3.7 years) than men (2.2 years).
- Thirty percent of sixty-five-year-olds may never need long-term care, but 20 percent will need it for more than five years.

The statistics are a call for readiness and action. This call must be answered by financial firms by partnering with health care facilities, nursing homes, and senior living communities. The issue of concern is that not enough people have insurance contracts, which they would ideally borrow against later in life to help fund their long-term care needs. While they are still insurable, we suggest financing the right amount of coverage not only to protect your family after you're gone, but also to ensure the right amount of coverage to supplement the high expenses one may bear in future long-term care.

---

[332] "How Much Care Will You Need?" *LongTermCare.gov*, 18 February 2020, https://acl.gov/ltc/basic-needs/how-much-care-will-you-need

Premium financing[333] of such a plan is as easy as getting a mortgage on a home purchase. The process goes as follows:

1. A commercial bank lends funds, which the borrower then uses to pay premiums.
2. The pledging of that life insurance policy serves as a main source of collateral for the loan.
3. The loan is repaid, per the terms of the contract, using the policy's cash value, insurance benefit, or other assets.

The benefits are:

- The ability to obtain life insurance policies with a large face value without liquidating assets.
- Protection from potential gift taxes.
- The cash value of the life insurance policy may exceed the value of the loan and interest.
- The loan can cover multiple policies.
- Borrowers do not have to pay short-term capital gains from liquidating assets to pay premiums.
- The money creates liquidity for managing estate tax obligations.
- Borrowers can free up assets for other purchases.

Insurance entrepreneurs must bring opportunity to these communities. They must offer tax-free retirement income strategies and principal-protected insurance contracts, among other more sophisticated risk management solutions.

Insurance entrepreneurs must bring economic freedom to communities in Opportunity Zones. Choice is essential to the survival and success of these communities. And the incentives for every-

---

333 "Premium financing." *Lincoln Financial Group*, www.lincolnfinancial.com/public/professionals/productsandinsights/individuallifeinsurance/growyourbusiness/premiumfinancing

one—including insurance entrepreneurs and residents—are several and substantial.

Seizing these opportunities is a way to repair the breach and raise up the foundations of many generations, thus restoring the lives and dignity of our fellow citizens.

Opportunity Zones are a grant to uplift the world, and insurance service-related businesses in these zones can help a generation of Americans ill prepared to fund their retirements and long-term care needs.

FINALE

"No book can ever be finished. While working on it we learn just enough to find it immature the moment we turn away from it."

—Karl Popper, *The Open Society and Its Enemies: The Spell of Plato*

I am a New Yorker who lives in the Sunshine State, and a Floridian who is at home in Florida, Missouri—not because I am from Mark Twain's hometown, but because I believe in the words of the Show Me State.

I believe every investor should be a resident of the Tell Me Everything in Advance State—a place where disclosure is full and free—rather than a habitué of the Trust Me State, where proof is optional and verification impossible.

What Twain writes in *The Gilded Age*[334] defies age. He translates the folly of wasteful and ridiculous excess, saying:

Beautiful credit! The foundation of modern society. Who shall say that this is not the golden age of mutual trust, of unlimited reliance upon human promises? That is a peculiar condition of

---

334 Twain, Mark and Charles Dudley Warner. (1873). *The Gilded Age: A Tale of Today.* Gunterberg.org. https://gutenberg.org/ebooks/3178

society which enables a whole nation to instantly recognize point and meaning in the familiar newspaper anecdote, which puts into the mouth of a distinguished speculator in lands and mines this remark: 'I wasn't worth a cent two years ago, and now I owe two million dollars.'

Instead of gilding gold and putting gold on top of gold, Twain mines the words for William Goldman to claim as his own, for the character says, "Nobody knows anything, really, you know, and a woman can guess a good deal nearer than a man."

Twain saw prosperity descend into panic—twice. He finished *The Gilded Age* in the spring of 1873, four months before the day of the fall or two days before the beginning of fall, when, on September 20, 1873, the New York Stock Exchange closed its doors for ten days. He saw the start of the first Great Depression, now known as the Panic of 1873.

He saw the lesson that history teaches via the Panic of 1893. He saw the scene in *Frank Leslie's Illustrated Newspaper*, of a mob[335] storming the Fourth National Bank, on October 4, 1873.

He saw a similar scene[336] on May 9, 1893, of panicked stockbrokers on the floor of the New York Stock Exchange. An illustration of the open outcry system, of traders clutching sell orders and of a broker writing out market orders, the scene features specialists trading beneath mounted street signs and hanging scrolls for Unlisted Securities and Union Pacific.

---

[335] Panic of 1873 Image: Panic of 1873 bank run [Photograph]. Retrieved from Wikimedia Commons: https://en.wikipedia.org/wiki/Panic_of_1873#/media/File%3APanic_of_1873_bank_run.jpg

[336] Panic of 1893 Image: Panic at the NYSE, 5 May 1893 [Photograph]. Retrieved from Wikimedia Commons: https://en.wikipedia.org/wiki/Panic_of_1893#/media/File%3APanic_at_the_NYSE_5_May_1893_cph.3b13869.jpg

But for the venue, the illustration looks like wheedling among the wooly, or a portrait of traders with white mutton chops and walrus mustaches.

But for the top hats and morning coats, the illustration looks like gentlemen jawing for redress.

But for the names, the culprits remain the same.

What is different is the speed with which panic spreads.

All other differences notwithstanding, little else changes, as Twain writes in his letter[337] to Helen Keller:

It takes a thousand men to invent a telegraph, or a steam engine, or a phonograph, or a photograph, or a telephone or any other important thing—and the last man gets the credit and we forget the others. He added his little mite—that is all he did. These object lessons should teach us that ninety-nine parts of all things that proceed from the intellect are plagiarisms, pure and simple; and the lesson ought to make us modest. But nothing can do that.

Nothing can change the material nature of man, for nothing so radical exists to change our physical existence and turn us to gods.

But at the same time, nothing prevents us from aspiring to know the immaterial world of grace and universal truth.

The import of this book is in the impact it has on people from all stations of life.

I've translated words into works in hopes that this book is my contribution to the world.

---

[337] Twain, Mark. "All Ideas Are Secondhand." *Lapham's Quarterly*, 17 March 1903, www.laphamsquarterly.org/memory/all-ideas-are-secondhand

I hope to repair the world, in keeping with the laws of my faith and with faith in the Creator of all mankind. I hope to give hope, so we may all rejoice in the goodness of the wise and the kindness of the able.

AFTERWORD

Jack Kent Mandel (JKM) was an arrow of light in a triangle of shadow.

He was blond and tan in a plaza filled with brown and gray, cutting through a monolith of modernism; countering drag with the lift of charisma; resisting the wind of rhetoric, of air made more turbulent by an heir to fortune and an inheritor of power, of a time made more tragic by the governor of the Empire State (Nelson Rockefeller) and the president of the United States (Lyndon Johnson); gliding past the past to arrive—to announce his arrival—at a former Air Force base; landing at his base of operations: Nassau Community College (NCC).

Students chased JKM, waving registration forms for him to sign. He signed the forms with the flourish of a rock star autographing album covers, initializing his approval without prior approval. When he was done, his class was held in the largest classroom on campus, a 400-seat theater reserved for banquets, film festivals, and award ceremonies.

He was a professor of marketing and the most direct practitioner of direct marketing. He taught sports marketing and made a sport of marketing himself throughout Long Island, New York.

JKM was also a publisher[338], correspondent[339], publicist[340], and connector[341]. Language was his currency, barter his means of transaction, and persistence his stock-in-trade.

He was the only civilian with house accounts at his choice of restaurants and retailers, carrying his collections—parcels of meat, fish, and poultry wrapped in butcher paper—while tipping workers to stack his dry cleaning in the trunk of his convertible.

At home, he filed dispatches[342] from his imagination.

He typed letters to moguls, magnates, and even a nude model.

He convinced the promoters of a repertory company of muscled giants to travel from Greenwich, Connecticut, to Garden City, New York.

He convinced Vince and Linda McMahon of the World Wrestling Federation (WWF, now WWE) to speak to his students.

He convinced the McMahons to visit his classroom, rather than the Nassau Coliseum.

Then he convinced the county to let him use the Coliseum as a classroom.

---

338 Nemy, Enid. "Discoveries." *New York Times*, 28 December 1977, www.nytimes.com/1977/12/28/archives/discoveries-come-to-a-party.html

339 News 12 Staff. "Retail expert gives tips for Amazon Prime Day shopping." *News 12*, 14 July 2019, https://bronx.news12.com/retail-expert-gives-tips-for-amazon-prime-day-shopping-40786279

340 "Marketing students meet the pros." *Campus News*, 13 March 2019, https://cccnews.info/2019/03/13/marketing-students-meet-the-pros/

341 City Desk. "County exec visits NCC class." *Campus News*, 9 December 2019, https://cccnews.info/2019/12/09/county-exec-visits-ncc-class/

342 LIBN Staff. "Jack the nimble." *Business Wire*, 10 May 2002, https://libn.com/2002/05/10/jack-the-nimble/

JKM convinced another resident of the Gold Coast, the founder and manager of a hedge fund, to commute every Friday from Westport, Connecticut, to NCC.

He convinced this person to teach a fifteen-week course—to teach JKM's course—so I could experience the pleasure of educating a classroom of young minds. JKM wanted me to have his sense of professional contentment, which he felt I was lacking. JKM knew that the day-to-day execution of a career in equities and seeing the inequities of finance was causing me great concern.

That he convinced his eldest son to teach this course, that his son accepted JKM's offer without consideration, that I did not reconsider the cost of forgoing any consideration whatsoever, including the cost of driving to and from Long Island to teach a three-hour course on marketing, is a testament to the will of my father, Jack Kent Mandel, aka Professor JKM of Long Island.

More impressive is the fact that I had to ask JKM permission to teach, that I had to come to him as a supplicant in need of a favor, that I had to thank him for the privilege of asking him for a favor while performing a series of rituals, from the presentation of gifts—including a bakery box tied with twine, inside of which laid a chocolate crumb cake—to the placement of his favorite lawn chair; that I had to stand in silence while JKM sat and sunned himself with his carcinogenic tanning reflector.

The silence made a minute seem like an hour, by which time I could have been in New York City.

Through the distortion of time, memories of all the times JKM had dismissed the city as a sight to view, not a site to visit, became cards in a flip book without a timeline. Such was the Mutoscope of my mind in which cards made with silver compounds were made from silver columns.

Such was the state of matter in my mind's eye in which the past was not even past, as one card reappeared without warning, as the cards of destiny and death revealed a singular catastrophe: the Tower card in the tarot representation of fire and ruin; the collapse of the Twin Towers.

But for the chance to start my own fund, but for the randomness of chance itself, chances are I would have died at my trading desk on the 104th floor of One World Trade Center.

My friends and colleagues at Cantor Fitzgerald died on that floor.

They died eighty-seven days before the sixtieth anniversary of a sudden and deliberate attack against America.

They died on September 11, 2001—a date that will live alongside December 7, 1941, in infamy.

In the years since 9/11, until the final day of his years, my father avoided New York City. Through years born of experience, during years borne from his experiences in the city, my father said little about the city.

My father spent four years riding the subway from Brooklyn to Manhattan. He graduated with a business degree from Baruch College, a constituent college of the City University of New York (CUNY). His professors encouraged him the entire way. And yet the reality of the times—the reality of religion-based bias by the Fortune 500 companies that he applied to work at—made it hard for him to get a job commensurate with his talent and skills.

He came from a blue-collar neighborhood, not a blue-blooded family. He studied at a college rich in academics, not a college for the rich. He was born in a home of the children of immigrants, not a house that employed them.

He broke the silence with these words.

"Good luck. After you teach this class, maybe you can write a book like I did," he said.

The catch in his throat, the quickness by which he rose from his chair and lowered his head without facing me, walking inside without saying goodbye—the understanding was clear.

"Your father loves you," my mother said when I shared what happened. "You know, he's never had a real teaching assistant or shared his lesson plans with anyone. On move-in day at Brandeis, after you unpacked, your father and I went to see the statue of Justice Brandeis. Along the way, we could not have been more than a few feet from the statue, because we saw the justice's robes flying in the wind; we saw a sense of motion in the sculpture. Then your father stopped. He pointed to a brick building—Ford Hall[343]—and said, 'Building H[344].' He meant *your* building looked like *his* building at NCC."

"Flash forward to move-in day at Brown, when your brother met his roommates. Your father left—he left the residence hall—to tour the Sciences Library[345], 'SciLi.' When I found him, I was more relieved than angry. I was plenty angry, too, until your father said, 'It's Building T[346], the Tower at Nassau. Same style.'

---

[343] Ford Hall Occupation: Ford Hall occupation. Retrieved from Brandeis University Archives & Special Collections: https://lts.brandeis.edu/research/archives-speccoll/exhibits/ford/index.html

[344] Martin, Paul R. III. "Walk Around—March 1, 2020." *Beneath the Shadow of Wings*, https://mitchelfield.weebly.com/walk-around-2020.html

[345] Sciences Library Photo: Brown University Sciences Library Providence [Photograph]. Retrieved from Wikimedia Commons: https://en.wikipedia.org/wiki/Sciences_Library_(Brown_University)#/media/File%3ABrown_University_Sciences_Library_Providence.jpg

[346] Nassau Community College Photo: NCCC by Matthew Bisanz [Photograph]. Retrieved from Wikimedia Commons: https://en.wikipedia.org/wiki/Nassau_Community_College#/media/File%3ANCCC_by_Matthew_Bisanz.jpg.

"Jason, I swear, it was like that nighttime scene in *Breaking Away,*[347] when the father and son walk the grounds of Indiana University. The father says, 'I cut the stone for this building. I was proud of my work. And the buildings went up. When they were finished, the damnedest thing happened. It was like the buildings were too good for us. Nobody told us that. It just felt uncomfortable, that's all.'

"Your father did not have to tell me either. I realized what those buildings—the buildings at Brandeis and Brown—meant to your father. Jason, he is proud of you and your brothers."

*

"A man tells his stories so many times that he becomes the stories. They live on after him, and in that way he becomes immortal."

—Will Bloom (Billy Crudup), *Big Fish*

Jack Kent Mandel[348] died on February 24, 2021.

His stories live on after him, through his sons and grandchildren and among his extended family of admirers and friends.

May his memory be a blessing.

---

[347] *Breaking Away*. Directed by Peter Yates, performances by Paul Dooley and Dennis Christopher, 20th Century Fox, 1979. YouTube, uploaded by Fritz Engstrom, 29 June 2018 https://youtu.be/qhiqjAAILGg

[348] Lauterbach, Jordan. "Jack Mandel, longtime Nassau Community College marketing professor, dies at 73." *Newsday*, 17 March 2021, www.newsday.com/long-island/obituaries/jack-mandel-obituary-1.50175980

MANDEL FAMILY OFFICE
Mandel Family Office
5255 N. Federal Highway
Suite 310
Boca Raton, FL 33487

Phone: (888) 379-0270
Fax: (561) 424-8050
Cell: (917) 603-2365
Email:
jason@themandelfamilyoffice.com
Website:
http://www.themandelfamilyoffice.com

SPECIALIZED SERVICES

Due Diligence and Performance Reviews
Analysis on existing asset managers and investment strategy alignment.

Tax Minimization and Efficiency
Elimination of capital gains/estate taxation and structuring of assets in an optimized manner.

Asset Protection and Tax-Free Cash Flow
Digital vaults and traditional structures designed to generate tax-free income.

Alternative Investment Management
Access to proprietary non-correlated investment solutions focused on asset-backed lending and arbitrage strategies.

Scan the code for additional content.

Printed in the USA
CPSIA information can be obtained
at www.ICGtesting.com
LVHW090227191123
764328LV00032B/1265/J

9 781956 914917